I0816376

GAME CHANGER

GAME CHANGER

PLAYING TO WIN AT XBOX, EA SPORTS, AND LIVERPOOL FC

PETER MOORE

LIVERPOOL UNIVERSITY PRESS

First published 2025 by
Liverpool University Press
4 Cambridge Street
Liverpool
L69 7ZU

British Library Cataloguing-in-Publication data
A British Library CIP record is available

The manufacturer's authorised representative in the EU for product safety is Easy Access System Europe, Mustamäe tee 50, 10621 Tallinn, Estonia https://easproject.com (gpsr.requests@easproject.com)

ISBN 978-1-83624-579-7 hardback

Typeset by Carnegie Book Production, Lancaster

Printed and bound by CPI Group (UK) Ltd, Croydon CR0 4YY.

To the city that raised me,
the game that saved me, and the
people who walked beside me.
This is our story.

CONTENTS

PROLOGUE

YOU CAN GO HOME AGAIN

On certain Saturdays, the alarm will go off at 4 a.m. in the dead of the California night. I am an early riser by nature, but not *that* early. The hills are pitch-black; I could just as well be getting up on the dark side of the moon.

I have learned to move with economy and purpose at this ungodly hour. I pad quietly to the kitchen to start the coffee, and then I stretch a bit, and move stealthily toward the living room.

I'm still groggy, but by 4:25 a.m. I'm sitting down with my usual morning caffeine delivery system—latte, non-fat milk, double shot—and a rising sense of anticipation. I turn on the widescreen, and magically there it is, 5,282 miles away:

Anfield.

No matter the dodgy weather in England—whether it's raining or snowing, sunny or overcast—the pitch always looks resplendent on TV, and as Liverpool Football Club enters to supporters singing "You'll Never Walk Alone," I am right back home, in almost every meaningful sense of the word, even though I'm watching from half a world away.

When kickoff is at 12:30 p.m. in the UK, this is when I'm up in California, to accommodate the eight-hour time difference. I realize, of course, that none of this is strictly necessary. I have friends, diehard Liverpool FC fans every bit as devoted as I am, who choose to DVR these early kickoffs, then rise at a more reasonable hour, and watch after they've had a decent night's sleep. For some reason, though, I feel compelled to be there in real time, to watch the action as it's happening, part of a complicated compact I have with my club.

Maybe it's because, even after all these years, the ability to simply watch still feels like such a privilege. I spent my childhood in the UK, where football was almost literally never on television, and then the '80s and '90s in America where the entire sport was treated like something of a rumor. Now I have arrived at this moment in globalization, technology, and consumer choice when I am able to see every match every season, all while being sheepishly aware that, due to domestic TV blackouts, it is actually far easier to watch every Liverpool game in the States than it is in Liverpool itself.

There is more to life than football, and I've had the good fortune to experience much of it across the span of seven decades. But this sport and this club has been the glue, has allowed my life to make a kind of sense, even when at times I wasn't sure it made any.

Now that the story makes more sense, I'm ready to tell it. Though I was born in Liverpool and spent my teenage years in Wales, I visited the United States for the first time at the age of 23, and that sent me on a different path—or more accurately on a *variety* of different paths.

I loved America instantly, loved all the ways it was different—less entrenched, more optimistic, more casual, less cynical, more friendly—than the United Kingdom of that time. I was energized and transformed, and did everything I could to realize my own Scouse version of the American Dream. For nearly forty years, I worked my way through various industries, first in the athletic footwear market, selling Patrick shoes out of the back of my car in California, and then eventually as a senior vice-president for Reebok in Massachusetts. That job took me to remote, far-flung countries, and also to the pinnacle of big-time sports, from Olympic Games to World Cups.

Then I took a radically different tack and moved back

to California, where I soon found myself running Sega of America, launching the Sega Dreamcast, and playing a key role in the video-game industry, a business I had known next to nothing about seven months earlier. Later I was hired away by Microsoft and moved to suburban Seattle to help launch the Xbox 360 and spend several years in the belly of the Microsoft beast. From there, I took another job back in California, as one of the executives running Electronic Arts, and spent more than a decade helping to expand the reach of the company that proudly declares, "It's in the Game."

Throughout those years, even as I was raising a family and becoming more American in my outlook, attitudes, and dress, a common thread in each different post was the compulsion to keep tabs on Liverpool FC, and return to Liverpool whenever I could visit, to sit in the stands and cheer on the Mighty Reds.

Then came the most unusual job offer of all—to come back to Liverpool in 2017 as the CEO of Liverpool Football Club, literally the only job that would make me leave the US. It was Thomas Wolfe who said "You Can't Go Home Again," but I was determined to prove him wrong. For the next three and a half years, I threw myself into that job, and did it quite well, I believe—though I would leave that post in the fall of 2020 and return again to the United States.

Through the twists and turns and occasional missteps of my career, I learned some things about America and the United Kingdom, about leadership and business and sports, about love and responsibility and the importance of family, and about the vitality and necessity of play in all its many forms. I also learned that even when all your dreams come true, it still doesn't matter if you haven't found the right person to share those dreams with.

In the process, I'm sure I've become quite American, at least in the eyes of my childhood mates back in the UK. And yet, when that alarm goes off at 4 in the morning, I know who I am, and I know where I feel most at home, even if only in spirit. And the thing that is clear to me is that being from Liverpool—and *of* Liverpool—made all the other things possible.

CHAPTER ONE

HALF A CROWN

My story starts well before I do, and revolves around two things that would become central to my life: football and the art of conversation.

The seminal event occurred in 1950 on a dreary, drizzly Sunday morning in Liverpool—which is to say, a typical Sunday morning in Liverpool. This is Britain after the war, still recovering and rebuilding, queues and shortages and austerity everywhere, lives being rebuilt, things inching back toward something like normalcy.

In bucolic Garston Park in gritty south Liverpool, a neighborhood football match is taking place. Most of the men are huffing up and down the pitch with their pants rolled up to the shins, dress shirts off, with braces over their undershirts. A few dozen friends and relations are standing and lounging about, watching the action, and enjoying a day away from the work grind.

The strapping Arnie Moore is out there on the pitch, heard as well as seen. Arnie is instantly noticeable—he's everybody's mate, a hail fellow well met, and handsome to boot. On this day, he has invited out a young woman he fancies, the lovely Marilyn Bree, to watch him in action. She is a fetching nurse, and quite a contrast to the voluble Arnie. She's petite, reserved, and self-possessed, but thinks enough of Arnie that she's agreed to come and watch him in action.

But now sidling up to Marilyn, among the smattering of pitchside observers, is Arnie's older, shorter, arguably less physically attractive brother, Terry Moore. Terry was born with a cleft palate and a harelip, so he's sported a mustache ever since he was old enough to grow one. His speech is a peculiar combination of Scouse lisp and nasal, reedy rasp, meaning you sort of have to know him to understand a single word he's saying.

Though humble in appearance, Terry possesses pocket aces. He's a student of human nature, adept at drawing people out of their shells, and a championship listener. All these talents will come in handy in future years, and on this day they will alter the course of multiple lives.

While Arnie runs up and down the field—fancying himself as the classic box-to-box midfielder, yelling out encouragement and expletives in equal measure—his brother begins chatting with Marilyn Bree. Terry isn't boastful or pushy or overly familiar, but he exhibits genuine interest, and he clearly has the gift of the gab. He finds out that everyone calls her Mal, and that she works at Alder Hey Children's Hospital.

What seems impossible in the moment makes more sense later on. It transpires that the dashing, likable Arnie Moore is great fun at parties, but not the most reliable bloke in the world. And after living through the Great Depression and World War II, Mal Bree is quite keen on reliability and consistency. In the diminutive brother conversing with her that morning, she senses a spark.

In the weeks ahead, she finds herself drawn to Terry's aura of unshowy steadfastness. He soon learns that her closest friends call her "Olive Oyl," because she has the same slim figure as Popeye's girlfriend. Terry turns out to be a good dancer and that helps. He is also eminently sensible, predictable, and sincere in his devotion. These things help even more.

The rest is history and an emphatic reminder that everything's fair in love and war. And that is the best explanation that survives about how the man who would become my father managed to steal the affections of the woman who would become my mother from his own handsome younger brother. With no hard feelings.

Therein resides a larger truth. That day in Garston Park, Terry Moore had come out to watch his brother play football. Then, at some point after meeting Marilyn, he sensed an opportunity and he took it. Recognizing your moment and grabbing it—having the audacity and wherewithal to talk yourself into (and, when necessary, out of) almost any situation—is a distinctly Liverpudlian trait.

It's also one that, for better or worse, I would inherit.

◆

Terry and Mal. It was an unlikely pairing, made more so by the fact that the Bree family came from good middle-class stock, while the Moores were a decidedly working-class outfit, though like typical Scousers they weren't afraid of taking shots on goal in life to see if one would find the back of the net.

The Brees might have been middle class, but they were hardly stodgy. My maternal great-grandfather, Charles Shute, had been a man of some renown in Liverpool. Of Irish heritage, like so many Liverpudlians of this era, he went by the stage name Charles Sandy, and teamed with another comic, Charles Carl, in a variety of stage endeavors. "Sandy & Carl" were a partner act—they played comedic routines on their own, but also took part in theatrical productions, usually in tandem. You might see Sandy & Carl playing the Silly Billy and Simon Softcake characters in a farcical rendition of *Jack & the Beanstalk* in the late 1890s, or in the supporting roles as the Emperor's attendants, Ping and Pong, in a Christmas Eve pantomime production of *Aladdin* in Bradford in 1903.

Charles Shute and his wife Martha emigrated to the United States in 1912, perhaps in hopes of bringing his talents to the American vaudeville stage. In the summer of 1928, they were joined by their daughter Marie and her husband, Sydney Bree. Syd was a veteran merchant seaman who'd been in the Royal Navy in World War I, and came to the States hoping to find steady work. Within a year, he was working as a rigger on the railroad.

Syd and Marie's first child, Marilyn Bree, was born on New Year's Day 1930 in Quincy, Massachusetts. But already by then, their immigrant dreams had collided with the stock-market crash and the onset of the Depression. The Brees and baby Marilyn would soon return to England.

Things were no better in Europe, of course, with the shadow of Hitler and Nazi Germany looming over the continent. By the time my mother was 10, her father had been called back to duty in the Royal Navy. Syd Bree had a particularly harrowing experience in World War II as the Battle of the Atlantic raged and Hitler's *Kriegsmarine* picked off the convoys from the eastern US carrying much-needed supplies to the UK and the Soviet Union. He was aboard the armed merchant cruiser HMS *Forfar,* which took five torpedo strikes from a German U-99 sub off the coast of Ireland in December 1940. One hundred seventy-two men died in the attack, while only 21 survived to be rescued. Leaping into the ocean to escape the flames on board, Syd was retrieved by a British steam merchant, SS *Dunsley,* only to have that ship subsequently torpedoed by German U-47s later the same day. Talk about a bad day at the office—on ships taking fire from the Germans twice in the same day, he somehow lived to tell the tale. He soon returned to battle, as the chief petty officer on a coastal patrol ship. After the war, Syd would lead a much less adventuresome life, going back to work for Canadian Pacific Steamships, serving as a warrant boatswain on ships like RMS *Empress of Scotland.*

The Moores were from a more decidedly hardscrabble background. There had been a time when the Moore family were prosperous ropemakers—a good vocation in a port city—but the Industrial Revolution and the internal combustion engine was not kind to ropemakers. By the 1920s, the Moores were laborers who made their living with hard work and muscle. My grandfather Fred Moore was a blunt, barrel-chested crag of a man, who spent his adult life working on the docks when it was nothing but draining manual labor—lifting crates and trunks with hooks and jibs, to the point of exhaustion and often crippling physical injuries. Fred and others like him didn't have a union to protect them. He'd rise at 5 in the morning, then go down to the massive Garston docks hoping to get selected for work. When he wasn't working, Fred had a voracious appetite and made nightly trips to the pub—by the time I remember him, he had grown into a formidable man-mountain.

Fred and Emma Moore raised their six children near Garston Park, in a house called "Bedlam"—the term itself came from the shortened nickname for the old St. Mary's of Bethlehem mental hospital in London. It was a fitting name for a chaotic home. There weren't only the half-dozen kids, but also grandparents, multiple generations moving in and moving out. Some long-lost relative would get off a boat with five bottles of rum and stop by Bedlam for a homecoming celebration. There was lots of drinking and lots of singing, and my grandmother's piano hauled out from under the stairs whenever those two pleasures came together, which was often from the stories we heard.

My father never talked much about his childhood. Sensitive about his birth defect, he remained self-conscious, wary, and uncomfortable in large crowds, even in adulthood. He was around alcohol his whole life, but you'd be hard-pressed to find anyone who ever saw him drunk.

Terry Moore was working as an apprentice toolmaker at

BEA—British European Airways—when he was conscripted in March 1942 and saw combat with the 89th Light Anti-Aircraft Regiment of the Royal Artillery. For much of the war, he was stationed in London, operating the Swedish anti-aircraft Bofors 40mm guns. "The Bofors Boys" they were called, surrounded by sandbags, pointing their guns skyward as the Germans bombed the city. The Bofors 40mm guns were surprisingly effective, able to shoot three rounds in 12 seconds, and move to nearly a 90-degree angle to fire at enemy aircraft. Once the Germans were retreating into central Europe, my father later served in Italy, working his way up to staff sergeant. What's so striking about the pictures of him from that era is that he has the careworn, lined face of a weathered middle-aged man. He was barely 20.

He was demobilized—demobbed, as they called it—in 1946, and returned to Bedlam, in the bomb-ravaged city of his youth. Outside of London, Liverpool was the most heavily bombed city in Britain, with the bombs of the *Luftwaffe* claiming over 4,000 lives. He had helped save the world from the forces of fascism, and resided in a port of one of the world's great powers, yet he faced a life of precious few options. Terry was a wise man in many ways, but his dedication to the defense of his country, like that of so many of his generation, resulted in an education level not really advanced much beyond primary school. He'd never had the chance to learn cursive handwriting, so as an adult he was limited to a precise but basic printing of all capital letters. After returning from the war, he found work as a freight clerk for BEA, before taking a similar job at Garston docks, where he worked not far from his father.

Around the same time, the precocious Marilyn Bree had started her nursing career, and her friends had started calling her "Mal." She had remained in Liverpool for much of the war, becoming wearily accustomed to the mad dash for the Anderson shelters whenever the air-raid sirens would go off.

At the end of the war, she would remember the resentment directed toward the American GIs—"overpaid, oversexed and over here," was the phrase common back then—living lavishly in an environment of severe austerity, when everything from meat to cheese to bread was being rationed. I remember her telling me she wore "liquid stockings": foundation makeup on the legs, and a drawn "seam" on the back. With great pride and even more resourcefulness, she used Bisto gravy as the paint for the seam. Desperate times, desperate measures.

Mal was unpretentious and level-headed. By 1948, she had started working at Alder Hey in West Derby. It was cutting-edge hospital in that era, with the first neonatal intensive care unit in all of Britain. Courted by many, she fell into a potentially serious relationship with a doctor, which many in her family thought might lead to marriage. But she eventually broke it off because, as she confided in friends and family, the man was an alcoholic. So she was young, accomplished, and eligible when she ventured out to Garston Park that day in 1950 to watch Arnie Moore in action, only to have her head turned by Terry.

It was not a long courtship; maybe nine months or a year tops. They were married in the spring of 1951, and moved into her parents' flat at 14B Hurstlyn Road in south Liverpool. There is a picture of Terry and Mal from this period, taken not long after their wedding day. They're standing in front of the ornate doors at St. George's Hall in Liverpool. They are young and in love; you can see the pride in his face, the amusement and enjoyment in hers (there were not many dress-up nights on the town). They are embarking on their own epic story.

There were setbacks early on. We never got the full story—so much in British life then involved measuring the considerable distance between what happened and what was discussed—but my parents' first child arrived stillborn, with club feet, at a time when the drug thalidomide was just being prescribed to treat morning sickness in pregnant mothers. (It would turn out that many of the women who took thalidomide gave birth to children with terrible deformities; the medication was eventually banned.)

Terry was still working on the docks when Mal got pregnant a second time. Then, perhaps because they were being unusually cautious, I was born in a hospital—Sefton General— on March 16, 1955. Thirteen months later, my brother Andy was born. That didn't quite make us "Irish twins," but it did mean we grew up nearly inseparable, sharing a room and all manner of life experiences.

Given the limited range of possibilities for a woman in Britain in the middle of the twentieth century, my mother was both skilled and successful. After Andy was born, my mum went back to work at Alder Hey to help pay the bills. When my mum would come home from a hospital shift at 8 p.m., my dad would prop Andy and me up in the living-room window to see her coming down Hurstlyn Road, a spring in her step, carrying a Milky Way bar as a treat for her boys.

She was making a bet on my father, and their future together. It may have initially looked to outsiders like she had picked the wrong horse. For a time after their marriage, our family lived with our grandparents, while my dad continued working at the Garston docks. It was less physically taxing than the work that his father did, but no less spiritually draining.

My father longed for a more promising career, and what he wanted to do more than anything was run his own pub. In England in the '50s, this was not as easy as renting a storefront and pouring drinks. Before one could be a licensee—the official operator of a pub, approved by authorities with one's name over the door—you had to work your way up.

Through the local Bent's Brewery, he jumped at the opportunity to serve as a manager at a corner pub just off the main drag of Scotland Road—Scotty Road to the locals—called the Dryden Arms, on the corner of Great Homer Street and Dryden Street in central Liverpool. The Dryden Arms was nondescript, one of those classic pub-on-every-corner establishments so common at the time. Located next to the well-established Hewlett's butcher's shop, it had steady business. But the hours were poor, the travel from south Liverpool was long, and my father was not the official licensee of the establishment; he took orders from Bent's.

It was perhaps here, during those very early formative years, that I first witnessed the unrelenting work ethic and dogged determination of those born on the banks of the Mersey. Come rain or shine the "barrow girls"—as in wheelbarrow—would push their wooden carts, laden with fruit and vegetables, up and down the gritty streets that conjoined Scotland Road and Great Homer Street. Typically, these were not girls at all but rather older women, seemingly forged in iron, faces etched with the travails of a lifetime of physical toil. I would occasionally see them in the mornings, bundled in heavy woolen coats and shawls protecting their heads from the unrelenting rain and bitter cold. They would gather on those gray mornings in front of the Dryden Arms, exchange pleasantries and gossip, then set off to the north and west, calling on homes and shops, peddling their wares in what even to my callow eyes seemed a brutally hard way for a woman to make a living.

While there was hard work just outside the Dryden Arms, there was hard drinking inside. My mother would long remember her first trip to the pub. She dressed for the occasion, wearing a nice dress and four-inch heels. Then she negotiated the cobblestone streets, and walked in to a full house of carousing workers, when Terry spoke up.

"No language! No more!," he barked. "This is my wife."

Her first thought was that she wanted nothing to do with the place. And yet. As Terry embarked on his new endeavor,

Marilyn was by his side, spending weeks scrubbing down every surface, making it presentable. Behind the bar, Terry was comfortable, and soon developed a following. Within a year, the family moved closer to the pub, to a flat around the corner. But the location was less than ideal, and the pub itself didn't have much going for it. Soon, Bent's offered my father a promotion, to manage a larger, free-standing pub, the Gay Cavalier in south Liverpool. It was a step up in some respects—there was accommodation right above the pub for the growing family to live in—but a step back in another.

The Gay Cavalier was located maybe fifty yards away from Speke Road Gardens council housing. These were planned tenements—densely packed four-story buildings nicknamed The Tennies—erected in 1933 as a means to solve housing shortages. Inevitably, it was the poorest families that wound up there, and throwing that many people together, with scarcely any opportunity for upward mobility, was a recipe for crime and horrific violence. Adding to the mix, you'd have merchant seaman from all over—Asia, Africa, Europe, the Americas—stopping in to let off steam. Weeks or months at sea makes for lots of steam to let off.

This was the clientele my father served on a daily basis. The Gay Cav, as they called it, was a bustling, throbbing organism, demanding his nearly constant attention. Among my earliest visions are my father coming up the stairs to the lodgings above the Gay Cav, his white shirt bloodied, because he'd had to go over the bar to intercede in one melee or another.

My fourth year would remain indelible. Grandpa Sydney Bree had retired, and he and Marie—Nana Bree—had purchased a caravan in Conway, North Wales. One night, Syd went out drinking with a cousin, and on the way back to the caravan site, the car they were in crashed into a tree and Syd was killed. In their younger days, Terry and Mal had

had to move in with her parents. Now the tables were turned, and Nana Bree would soon move in with us.

◆

That was the most momentous event of that year, but it wasn't the most memorable for me. That occurred Saturday morning, November 21, 1959. I was almost five. My father came into Andy's and my bedroom that morning and announced, "Okay, it's like this: I'm going to give one of you half a crown, and take the other one with me to Anfield, to watch the football."

Both my brother's eyes and my eyes lit up, for entirely different reasons. Half a crown was two shillings and sixpence, which was a fortune for a youngster in those days. Andy had already developed a sweet tooth, and enough of a head for numbers to realize that half a crown could buy an impressive assortment of sweets from the local confectioner. Neither of us remembers who answered first, but the choices were clear in an instant. Andy was going to the sweets shop to get several "Lucky Bags," the packets containing treats and the odd toy; I was going to the football match.

Kickoff was at 3:15, so I waited an eternity that day, deciding what to wear, wondering when we could leave. The anticipation was a kind of torment. I knew I was a Liverpool supporter, I'd seen the Liverpool team picture that my father kept behind the bar, I'd heard him speak glowingly of the brilliant winger Billy Liddell. But I'd never actually *seen* Liverpool Football Club in action. In those days, the only soccer match that was telecast live was the FA Cup Final, which Liverpool—then languishing in the English Second Division— hadn't made since five years before I was born. Not that we had a TV to watch it on.

That afternoon, one of my father's bar patrons picked us up

for the drive to Anfield. I was wearing the inevitable duffel coat with toggles across the chest—imagine a four-year-old dressed like Paddington Bear—and while I can't swear to it, I'm pretty sure that outside Anfield, my dad brought me a rosette, a red-and-white ribbon, with the Liver bird in the center.

As we neared the stadium there was the inevitable stop at a nearby pub, then we crossed the street amid the bustling crowd to the front gates. I held my father's hand, looking around wide-eyed at the bobbies sitting atop their massive horses.

"If he lifts his tail, son, get out of the way," advised my dad.

I can still remember whisking through the turnstile and then catching a glimpse of the brilliant green of the pitch. We made our way to the paddock area at Anfield—what those who've been there now will recognize as the Sir Kenny Dalglish stand. It was a standing area for an older, tamer crowd, more orderly than the febrile, pulsing organism that was the Kop.

Liverpool then wore red shirts and white shorts, with white socks with red trim. As the starting XI emerged from the tunnel to walk onto the pitch, the captain Ronnie Moran kicked a ball out ahead of them—it being 1959, the ball was still the old, orangish-brown leather football (caseys, they were called)—to a boisterous cheer from the stands.

I remember being surrounded by tall men smoking and swearing, seeing flashes of the green pitch through the forest of dark coats. Recalling his first game in his memoir *Fever Pitch*—an Arsenal match in the late '60s—the writer Nick Hornby would remark about the comprehensive maleness of the scene ("I'd heard those words before, but never by adults and never at that volume"). That was exactly the feel of the match at Anfield. It was, let's say, not a place frequented by women, and I don't remember a single female in the paddock area.

The game itself was a chaotic adventure. Liverpool were up 1–0 and 2–1, but down 3–2 by halftime. During the interval, my dad and I worked through the crowd for a cup of Bovril for me, and a cup of tea for him. Back in the paddock, we watched the tin numbered plates go up on the hand-operated scoreboard, providing updates for other matches around the country. The matches were listed in alphabetical order in the program, with the corresponding score posted at halftime for each letter. So there were cheers at the report of Everton falling away at Spurs, and disappointed murmurs about Manchester United thrashing Luton Town.

The paddock was at once a wonderful and terrible place to watch. You were nearly at pitch level, so it was very difficult to see what was going on at either end of the pitch. But you were so close to the players when the action came by that you could hear the shouts from teammate to teammate, even smell the wintergreen liniment the players routinely rubbed on their legs.

In the second half, Liverpool's Dave Hickson equalized in the 50th minute before Fred Morris's second goal of the match won it in the 81st minute. The entire experience was mesmerizing. I returned home transformed. I'm sure I spent more time kicking the ball around the week after than I ever had before, imagining myself as one of my new heroes who I had finally witnessed in the flesh on that fateful day, one that would spark the love affair that would last a lifetime.

I quickly became more attuned to the fixture list, and cognizant of when the Reds were playing, whether it was home or away. After a while, I was going with my dad to pick up the football edition of the local paper, the Saturday evening pink *Football Echo*, with late-breaking news on all the scores, somehow delivered onto the streets within hours of the final whistles around the country. I soon learned the paper's shorthand: The illustration of the Kopite on the header—a sort of superfan in a bobble hat, a scarf, a rosette, and a rattle—was either waving his rattle and dancing (which meant Liverpool won) or with his head downcast (which mean we'd lost), and the Toffee Lady on the other side of the page would be dancing a jig with her umbrella (an Everton win) or with her head down (an Everton loss).

But on that Saturday afternoon, all I knew for sure was that it was the most exciting thing I'd ever experienced in my life. When we got home, my mother wanted to know how I liked it, while Andy was in his room, jealously guarding his bag of sweets.

I had just one question for my father: "When do we go back again?"

CHAPTER TWO

THE RED LION

Today, Liverpool is a resplendent jewel of a cosmopolitan city, a cultural capital that blends modernity with tradition in a way that's unique. But when I was growing up in the early '60s, it was a hurting place, a city still recovering from the war and adjusting to its changing role in the modern world. Once the world's largest shipping port, it had struggled to cope with a new age of increasing automotive and air mobility. After the beating the city took from the German blitzkrieg in World War II, Liverpool in the '50s and '60s was still littered with wrecked "bombdies"—bombed-out homes—lining some of the streets. The memoirist Lorna Sage would describe a city "pocked with bomb sites … a great emptiness where swathes of streets had been razed to the ground." Even to this day, St. Luke's Church, at the top of Bold Street, is a shell without a roof, having been badly damaged by a German firebomb in 1941 and never repaired, a standing monument to those of the city who perished during the blitzkrieg. (To every Liverpudlian, it's known as the Bombed-Out Church, now a unique venue for concerts and summer events.)

The lack of housing and diminishing commerce put a further strain on social services, and that meant even more people crowded into the tenements of Speke Road Gardens, with precious few employment opportunities for the tenants there. The Gay Cav was doing a healthy business, but every day was an ordeal. Frustrated Speke Road Gardens residents seeking work would come in, inevitably crossing paths with frustrated workers from the docks or the airport or the Bryant

& May match factory across the street. The different groups often took their frustrations out on each other, with stupid arguments escalating into fistfights, drunken brawls starting in the tavern then spilling out into the car park. I particularly remember the Orange marches each July, with members of the Protestant Orange Lodges marching down Speke Road, right past the tenements, which housed their fair share of Catholics. They were viewed as sectarian celebrations of the defeat of Irish Catholicism, and inevitably a brick or two was thrown, signaling the onset of all-out brawls. I was eight years old, and I remember being frightened each and every day about the simmering mayhem that was always lingering close to the surface of life in the Gay Cav.

This was the Liverpool of my youth. The Merseyside signposts that would become legendary were back then just a part of our mundane daily existence. The Cavern Club opened in an old bomb shelter in 1957. My brother and I would pass by the gates of Strawberry Field—the Salvation Army home for vulnerable children—on our way to school. We got our hair cut on Penny Lane, just around the way from the McCartney family, whom my parents knew in passing. In earlier days, Terry and Mal used to drink with Paul's parents down at the Heath Hotel. (My mother once casually mentioned that she had babysat Paul when he was younger.)

But in the main, Liverpool was still down on its luck in the early '60s, when the emergence of the Beatles provided a bracing bright light in an otherwise grim environment. My brother Andy would recall a trip to the dentist around 1963 that was delayed by a massive crowd of teenage girls on a street corner. The Fab Four were back in town, and Beatlemania was exploding.

◆

After my younger brother Phil was born in 1961, we had the six people—me, Andy, Phil, my mum and dad, and Nana Bree—all living over the Gay Cavalier.

Two things were true. Our growing family was a product of Liverpool. We had Liverpool in our DNA. For the rest of our lives, we would be characterized and defined by our Scouse roots. Yet raising a family while managing the Gay Cav was a hard life, and not getting any easier. At that moment, my parents felt like they needed to get us out of Liverpool, for their sake and ours. We would forever remain Liverpudlians at heart. But not, for the time being, in Liverpool.

My dad was offered the opportunity not only to manage but also be the licensee of a pub called the Red Lion in North Wales. My parents took out a loan to afford the lease on the pub, staking their future and ours on its success. One day in 1964, Terry received a letter from the licensing authority in Denbighshire, a county in Wales: "We have received your application to come to The Red Lion in Marford as the licensee, and it will be reviewed." It was around then that he gave us the news of the pending move. Geographically, it was not a great distance. Marford, just outside of Wrexham, was only 32 miles south of Liverpool. And yet it was a world away. A different pub, in a different setting, in a different country.

The Red Lion, a property of Burtonwood Brewery, was housed in an old hotel, refashioned as a pub, with a small kitchen in the back and a three-bedroom home upstairs. We met the first regular of the Red Lion literally the moment the family arrived in Marford, and walked into the establishment the first time. There, sitting at the bar, was Gerry "Doddy" Dodd, whose vocation was that of the eternal trader—the timeless principle of "buy for £1, sell for £2"—dealing in everything from underwear to cologne to dodgy knock-off watches, often from the boot of his car. The pub was Doddy's stage and he gave shows daily and nightly, holding forth with opinions, one-liners, jokes, and a bristling running monologue about the state of the world.

At the beginning, there weren't many others. On my dad's official first day of business—"Terence Moore, Licensee" above the door—the locals were taking a wait-and-see attitude. He brought in all of £17.

But he had faith in the proposition, and in those first weeks in Marford my father began establishing himself as the new publican in town. The clientele grew steadily, an agreeable mixture of shift workers with a higher standard of living than the Speke Road residents, mixed in with a newly emerging professional class that was moving into the housing developments just north of Wrexham. This was the place my father felt most at home.

Away from the Red Lion, out in public, he could be a man of tics and insecurities—about his looks, his speech, even his stature. He also still bore the emotional scars of his anti-aircraft combat duty during the war. Whenever anyone remarked on a full moon, I could hear my father reflexively mutter under his breath, "Bomber's moon," vividly recalling those cloudless nights when German bombers could attack the cities of London and Liverpool at will. He never learned to drive a car, and even when riding in one, he had this idiosyncratic claustrophobia that meant he refused to fasten his seat-belt buckle, instead nervously holding it near but never in the clasp.

But in the four-foot square behind the bar at the Red Lion, Terry Moore was the master of his realm. Presiding over the social interaction, at once relaxed and attentive, he was in his element. It was his world, and the assembled masses—his family, the unruly gallery of regulars, passers-by, and occasional guests—were all just living in it.

Because my dad was a diehard, fiercely loyal Scouser embedded in Wales— "Scousewalians" was the popular term—the pub inevitably became known as a haven not only for Liverpool supporters, but football fans of all stripes. There was talk of horse racing and the latest politics, but most of the banter centered around football.

He kept a Liverpool team picture on the wall, updated each season. Terry would argue with everybody, about everything, most especially football. And he knew his football. Want to know the starting XI of Liverpool's 46/47 First Division champs? My dad could recite them. Need to settle an argument? My dad always had the latest edition of the *Rothmans Football Yearbook* behind the bar.

So people would come from all parts of Wrexham to argue with him about football. There was an aspect of theater to it; talking football—debating players and sides and managers—was his calling card. He once ruefully observed, "Every time Liverpool lose, I make a fortune," because all the Chelsea, Leeds, and United fans would come by to give him stick and hoot about the Reds' adversity.

Terry was an expert at finding common ground; if a new face came in who turned out to be a Newcastle supporter, and there was someone else at the bar who was an Arsenal fan, he would find a way to bring the two into conversation about the great FA Cup final of 1952.

What my father understood intuitively—I'm quite sure he never would have articulated it this way—was that football offered a civilized kind of tribalism, a way for people to come together and find common cause from diverse backgrounds. For years, my mum and dad's closest friends were a pair of Everton supporters, the dashing Jon Carr (known around town as "Man in a Suitcase," after the handsome actor Richard Bradford, who starred in the BBC series of the same name) and the elegant Joanne Carr, a handsome couple who'd recently moved to Marford. When Liverpool won the FA Cup in 1965, Terry needled Jon no end. And when Everton took the title a year later, he gleefully returned the favor. In fact, the first time I ever went to Goodison Park was with Jon Carr, who took me in 1968 in what I assume was an effort to convert me to the blue side of Merseyside. Despite the quality of that Everton squad that year, the effort was an exercise in futility.

In the late '60s, before the A483 motorway was built that bypassed the route, the Red Lion was right on the main road heading into Wrexham from the north. Whenever Wrexham played a team from the North, the football coaches would make their way on that road. Terry loved football, but didn't love the rollicking crowds—the Red Lion was primarily a haven for regulars. Terry took to putting up a sandwich board with a sign at the front of the car park, announcing "NO COACHES" every Saturday morning that Wrexham AFC had a home game. Usually this was sufficient, but one Saturday around lunchtime, he was tending the bar when a large coach pulled into the car park and literally ran over the NO COACHES sign.

"Jesus Christ!," exclaimed my father, before summoning my brother Andy to join him out front. "If we can keep the bastards from getting off, that'll be a lot easier than getting them back on." My father sprinted out to the coach—he did not, as a rule, do much running—and marched onto it as soon as the doors opened.

"What are you doing!?," he barked at the driver. "Did you not see the sign you just ran over that said NO COACHES?"

As the driver sputtered an apology, a drunken voice in the back of the coach bellowed, "Ah, fuck off, you Welsh bastard."

My father's eyes narrowed, and he turned his head and marched to the back of the coach, where in the midst of fifty or so already inebriated supporters, he faced up nose to nose with the drunk and said, "Call me bastard, but don't *ever* call me Welsh."

With that, he marched to the front of the coach, and said to the driver, "There's a pub a mile down the road called the Plough; go give them some shit."

◆

For the regulars and "the passing trade" who actually made it through the front door, the Red Lion offered a spacious, homey atmosphere. It was an L-shaped establishment, with the bar in the front when you walked in and, over to the left side, a spacious lounge, more often occupied by women. (Because the lounge had a handsome rug and more cushioned chairs, my father charged more for a drink in the lounge than for those standing or sitting in the bar area. The regulars steered well clear.) In between the bar area and the lounge was "the snug," a middle ground of sorts, often populated by a regular group of young middle managers from the area.

The hours were the same across the UK, and would define the rhythms of our lives: My mum and dad were up early. She was getting the place presentable (with the help of a cleaning woman named Glenys), setting out the ashtrays and the drip mats on each side of the square tables. My father would draw a morning bath and then be down to open the doors. The bar opened for business at 11:30 a.m., when Jackie "The Bread" Rowlands and other shift workers from Country Maid Bakery would stroll in after their 4 a.m.–11 a.m. shift, thirsty and sleep-deprived. It wasn't long before my mother started a lunch service in the back, cooking meals until 2 p.m. The bar started to slow down then, before the arrival of Angus "Gus" Jones, who lived just a few houses away, and invariably stopped in around closing time, ordering his second pint at 2:59, a minute before afternoon closing time. He then drank it slowly while my father fumed. Finally at 3:15, Gus would be on his way and my parents could retreat upstairs to rest. My father would read the six newspapers we received daily, poring over the horse racing form, reading up on the latest football news, and filling out the weekly football pool coupon sponsored by Littlewoods (it might as well have been a lottery—the "treble chance" called on selectors to pick eight draws out of a 55-game slate on Saturday, with the odds against doing that every bit as astronomical as it sounds). It seemed as though *everyone* bet the football pools, and for decades my father also placed regular, near-daily modest bets on horse racing and football, with a bookie in Liverpool whom he never met face to face. Dad's "handle" to that bookie was T-Rex, a nod to his name and location. On a good week, an envelope would come down from Merseyside. On a bad week, an envelope would head back north.

As my parents were acclimating to their new surroundings in the fall of 1964, I was doing the same, dropped into the bucolic Rossett Primary just north of Marford. It was a more provincial time, so even the small geographical distance between Liverpool and Marford made me and my accent exotic. Within a few days, I was given a nickname—"Scouse"—which stuck with me for ages. When Andy and I would return home from school, our parents were preparing for the longest part of their workday. My father would walk downstairs at 5:30 p.m. every day, and unbolt the door to find the perennials Charlie Wardell and Wilf Robinson waiting there. Charlie was "Charlie Chippie," who ran a fish and chip shop in nearby Gresford, and was a rabid Leeds United supporter. Wilf was a hard-working, hard-playing coal miner from the Gresford Colliery, just two miles down the road. The region was still haunted, three decades later, by the Gresford Colliery disaster of September 22, 1934, when an explosion and ensuing fire at the coal face claimed the lives of 266 miners and rescuers. The tragedy brought attention to the heinous working conditions in the mines, and eventually led to safety reforms, though far too late for those who were lost.

I can recall going down the hellish pit on a school trip in 1967, a visit that ensured I would pay more attention in school, in search of better occupational opportunities than those poor souls of decades earlier. Even in the '60s, it remained a brutal job. I can still see the blue lines on Wilf's burly hands and wrists, where cuts and scratches incurred while working at the coalface were infiltrated with coal dust.

The Red Lion was where Wilf and dozens of other regulars—the "professional alcoholics" who would populate the pub on a nightly basis—went for sanctuary and escape, finding there an egalitarian atmosphere of convivial banter.

◆

Then there was Terry's secret weapon—my mum. After a few years, as the lunch business got more successful, the Red Lion began offering dinner service as well. Mal was not a gourmet chef, but she was a solid English cook, unflappable and tireless, and she ruled the kitchen in the back of the Red Lion to precisely the same degree that my father ruled the pub in the front.

The Red Lion's menu was short and simple: there was a dish called "chipped rump steak," which was essentially a fancy variation on a hamburger which, for reasons lost to history, became known as a "monkey steak" in the family. It was the most popular dish, regularly outselling gammon steak, chicken and chips, shrimp scampi ("prawns in batter" on the menu), and a trout dish with a green pea placed carefully in the eye socket. My father would take an order at the bar, then call back to my mum on the bar phone: "Two monkeys on Table Six," and she would prepare the dish, then bring it out to the guests.

There were occasional skirmishes—a misunderstood order, monkey steaks delivered to the wrong table—and my father was convinced it was never his fault, and my mother was equally convinced it was never hers. It was not uncommon to hear one yelling at the other. But you could tell that they loved each other.

Once in a while, my mum would pass by my father on her way back to the kitchen, and he would surreptitiously slap her on the backside.

"Terry!," she would bark at him. He would smile and keep moving.

The work was ceaseless. All the orders were recorded in a giant logbook, then crossed off when they were sent to the tables. One evening, my mum cooked 142 different meals. This was well before the advent of "gastropubs," but her cooking was the difference-maker in growing the business in the face of so many other options in the area, with, at the time, at least two dozen pubs within a five-mile radius.

On weekend nights, and even some weeknights, the place was packed, with a raft of people up to the bar. I saw my father conduct proceedings with aplomb. Early evenings, when there were only a few regulars there, he could pay rapt attention to any of the filibusters going on by the bar. But when it got really crowded—full and raucous, standing three-deep at the bar, he possessed this otherworldly calm. It was always the same: As he was about to take an order from a patron, he'd look at the next person and reassure them, "I've got you," and then he would look at the person after that and say, "And you're next." It was a subtle touch, but it maintained order.

So people would come and have a good time. And come back. They would all blend together, in a cacophonous mix that at times could look effortless. The cigarette haze, combined with stale beer, and the trademark smell of the Polo mints my father would drop in the troughs of the urinal (why pay extra for air freshener?) gave the place an unmistakable aroma. As people would come to find out, if you'd been to the Red Lion, there was no point in saying you hadn't.

Downstairs, at 10:20 p.m., I'd hear my father ring the bell at the bar, the signal for last call, accompanied by a theatrical shout of "Last orders gentlemen, please!" At 10:30, he would dramatically throw a towel over the taps, signaling that no more drinks would be poured. At 10:40, he called for "drinking up" time, and people would down the remainder of their last pint. At 10:45, the customers would say their goodnights and leave, and my dad would lock up. Then for another half-hour or more, he'd clean the front, my mum would clean the back and they would trudge upstairs, exhausted.

Then the next morning, they'd get up and do it all over again.

This was their life—and because it was their life, it became the locus of our lives as well—and they did it, almost literally every day for the better part of twenty-two years.

Soon enough, sometime in 1965, Andy and I were co-opted for the cause. Not that we had much choice. Every Saturday morning, before breakfast, my brother and I would have to "bottle up," which meant taking the stock of Burtonwood Brewery bottles—lagers and stouts, tonics and bitters—from the storage room and placing them behind the bar. But never *just* that. We were each given a warm cloth, with which we'd wipe down each bottle, and then we'd place every bottle carefully in a column, like with like, label always facing out. Terry Moore insisted on a sense of order in his establishment.

We were a remarkably close-knit family in one respect, everyone working together under one roof. And yet, between my dad at the bar and my mum in the kitchen, it was not what you would call a typical domestic situation. In those early years at the Red Lion, Andy and I were sent to bed each night—bribed, actually—with a packet of crisps and a Coca-Cola. Not the ideal method to promote sleep hygiene, in retrospect, but a welcome regimen nonetheless. Our Nana Bree would look in on us to make sure the lights were out in the adjoining rooms in which Andy and I slept. But the walls were pasteboard, and we soon used a penknife to fashion a hole in the wall so we could converse into the wee hours.

Downstairs, we'd hear the shouts and laughter, the loud voices and the occasional flare-ups from the kitchen and the bar. It was the sound of people living; I enjoyed it, I absorbed it, and many a night I fell asleep to it.

◆

In the summer of 1966, on the last day of July, we did the most exotic of things. We brought our small black and white TV from upstairs and wheeled it into the pub on Sunday afternoon.

There, my dad and I and one or two regulars watched the 1966 World Cup Final. Coming within a generation after World War II, as England was reconstructing itself and seeking to recover its own sense of pre-war preeminence and prestige, the match—England v. West Germany—was freighted with great meaning.

On the morning of the final, Vincent Mulchrone, writing in the *Daily Mail*, counseled his English cohorts, "If the Germans beat us at our national game today, we can always console ourselves with the fact that we have twice beaten them at theirs." (To this day, whenever England faces Germany, you can still hear the chant of "Two World Wars, and one World Cup!," sung to the tune of "Camptown Races.")

My father remained staunchly English. To the end, he'd keep his Royal Artillery necktie—navy blue with a red lightning bolt—and don it on special occasions. He was especially proud that day. The English squad had three Liverpool players: Roger Hunt, Ian Callaghan, and Gerry Byrne, though only Hunt would start the final. Like the rest of our countrymen, we suffered through that game, cursing the Germans' late equalizer, then fretting through extra time before England's two goals finally clinched the Jules Rimet trophy. And no, I don't think Geoff Hurst's shot on goal that came down off the crossbar actually crossed the line, and yes, I will be forever grateful to the Russian linesman for thinking it had. There were toasts raised and anthems sung.

It would remain the signal moment in the history of English football, and I remember it all the more fondly because it occurred the same summer as an unexpected development—baked into the British class system at that time—changed my own life for the better.

CHAPTER THREE

GROVE PARK

I was 11 years old in the spring of 1966, adapting to life in Marford, playing football whenever I could, when I took the compulsory British "11-plus" exam, a broad-based aptitude test that would determine the route of my schooling.

Looking back, it's still sort of unbelievable that British schools presumed to determine the course of children's lives at the age of 11, sending some students on a path toward university education, allowing them to take O level and A level exams, while the rest were consigned to secondary moderns or technical schools, where they were denied the opportunity of a clear path to university but were instead directed to learn technical trades like bricklaying, electrical fitting, or plumbing. The system labeled children of my era as "successes" or "failures" at a ridiculously young age, creating psychological consequences and limiting opportunities for those who failed. It did not take into account late bloomers who would potentially mature academically in their early teen years, and students placed in secondary modern schools were often stigmatized and given fewer opportunities to progress academically.

But that was the stated goal of the 11-plus tests. The implications were momentous, and it's quite possible that if I had been fully aware of them, I'd have choked on the test. But I somehow passed. It was an upset of sorts, the bright side of the narrow-minded harshness of the British tripartite system. My mum was proud, my dad a bit surprised. I was the only one in my family who was given the opportunity to chart that course, and nearly sixty years later, the circumstances remain somewhat bewildering. I wasn't smarter than my siblings, but I suppose I was more studious. I didn't work any harder than they did, but I was more ambitious.

The tests revealed that I at least had the aptitude to follow the high road, the grammar school route. Like a proper Scouser, I saw my chance and took it. In the fall of 1966, that meant I landed in another strange realm, the forbidding world of Grove Park Grammar School for Boys, while my brother Andy wound up at Darland School, a secondary modern in Rossett.

The pattern of school days the next few years was set. Andy and I got up painfully early in the morning and raced downstairs to sit in front of the Red Lion's one source of heat, a gas fire in the wall that housed the dartboard, where we'd scoff down our bowl of porridge, then head out to our respective bus stops, across the street from each other. On the way out the door, we'd invariably have to pass inspection from my mother. If one of us had jam on our cheek—it was usually Andy, to be fair—she'd take her cigarette out of her mouth, spit into her handkerchief, then wipe it on his cheek until he was spotless. Thus cleansed, Andy would often venture to school smelling like an ashtray.

I'd wait for the local Crosville bus, which stopped right outside the Red Lion, and dropped me off at the King Street bus depot, about 300 yards from the doors of Grove Park Grammar School. It wasn't exactly Hogwarts, but it *was* an exacting, at times grimly staid all-boys grammar school. The dress code, like pretty much everything else at Grove Park, was strict: Black blazer with a red badge, gray shirt, black and red tie, black short pants for me and all the other first-formers (one had to earn his way to second form before having the option to cover your legs in the snowfall), and black Clarks shoes.

There were *so* many rules. No talking back. First-formers

had caps which had to be worn any time we stepped out of doors ("don't let the light hit your naked head"), but couldn't be worn inside.

Academically, we were thrown into the deep end, with nine subjects a day, lots of homework, and the sense that we were pieces of clay, there to be molded by the professors, known as "the masters." Almost all of the masters wore black robes, and most of them kept wooden rulers beneath their robes, with which to smack indifferent or intemperate students as they walked by their desks. If a student was getting cheeky, he might get a rap with a ruler or, if he was dozing in class, be jarred awake by a master throwing a board duster at him. The age-old edict of Spare the Rod, Spoil the Child might as well have been plastered over the ornamental grand doors at the entrance to the school, such was the prevalence of the masters delivering "six of the best" to pupils judged to be unruly.

My first term at Grove Park, I became collateral damage to this mindset. One of my classes was with an aging, pompous master, who for some reason was known to the students as "Hovis," a brand of hard brown bread prevalent in the UK working class. One day, the master was late to class and we were all milling around our desks—rather than sitting obediently at them, as required. When a fellow pupil saw the master approaching down the hallway toward the room, he said, "Sit down! Here comes Hovis!," and we all rushed back to our chairs.

It wasn't me. Honest.

But "Hovis" thought it was.

I was cuffed on the ear and summarily dragged to the staff room for my discipline. The art teacher Jimmy Johnson was there and Hovis summoned him to countersign the record of the beating, like some kind of corporal-punishment notary public. I was made to place my hands on the hot radiator, bend over, lift my blazer up so he could have a better shot at my backside, and absorb the caning. Hovis hadn't lost his fastball, but his aim was failing him, so in addition to getting whipped on my butt, I also weathered some vigorous shots on the back of my thighs.

I got home that afternoon a right mess. In some homes in Britain in those days, you might incur a beating at home as punishment for having taken a beating at school. But my mum saw the welts on my legs and was furious at the school, not me. She came with me to Grove Park the next day, demanded to see the headmaster, and engaged in what the diplomats describe as a "free and open exchange of views." The pompous headmaster apologized for the inaccuracy of the flogging, though not for the flogging itself. As it happened, I never got caned again. But I also learned to be far more careful—in my years at Grove Park, I was frequently on the periphery of trouble, but never quite in it. There was some internal governor that helped me rein it in when I sensed trouble.

The schoolwork was uniformly rigorous. Rows of desks with inkwells—all our writing was done with fountain pens. I learned (or attempted to learn) Latin and, eventually, five years of Welsh, which, with my Scouse accent, sounded more Klingon than Celtic. Every day, I'd come home with a much heavier homework load than I'd ever had before.

The saving grace was football. By the time I got to Grove Park, I was becoming a decent player. I lacked the speed and nose for the goal of the best forwards but was a robust right back, with dedication and a real zest for the game.

Among my closest friends at Grove Park was Chris Marsden. He was a year younger than me, the sort of football-playing prodigy who was better than anyone in his age group, and so was always moved up to the next age group, where he was often still the best player at that level. Chris had an easygoing manner, and a sense of whimsy that I liked. He also came from a great family. His sister Sharon was pretty and smart. Their dad, Harold—a hard-working trench-digger for the electric company—had once been on the books of Bolton Wanderers. Chris's family structure was more conventional than my own, and I enjoyed myself whenever I visited, even when Chris's little sister Sharon complained that I ate all their biscuits.

As Chris tells it, his first impressions of me was that I was some kind of Jack the Lad with all the gear, from floral-print shirts to flared trousers. There's some truth to that—it was the '70s, and when I didn't have to be in the Grove Park uniform, I wanted to be as far *out* of uniform as possible. But Chris and I forged a real friendship on the football field and eventually off it. He possessed what at the time seemed to me an otherworldly sense of field vision, 360 degrees of spatial awareness that I couldn't begin to match. My own skills were best exemplified down the single channel of the right back's track, moving up and back, overlapping when necessary, retreating on defense while always knowing the touchline served as an extra defender.

At Grove Park, both Chris and I fell under the spell of the man who, at that stage of my life, was as big of an influence as my father. He was Owen Maelor "O.M." Edwards, the physical education teacher and football coach at Grove Park, and everything—cool, relatable, respectful, attentive, carefree, funny—that all the other masters weren't. I loved my dad, and he taught me plenty, but I'd never had any desire to spend a lifetime tending bar. But in the composure, good humor, and sense of purpose that O.M. Edwards exhibited, I found a model to emulate, a north star for my teen years.

He was different than all the other teachers at Grove Park. Other masters wore robes; O.M. wore a tracksuit. Other masters scowled; O.M. laughed. Other masters called me Moore; O.M. called me Peter or "Scouse." He recognized my can-do attitude, and soon jokingly referred to me as "The Boy Who Would Never Say No." One sensed in his assured manner a world of carefree possibilities, vigor, fun, and sophistication. When he would sit in his office, smoking his pipe (an admittedly odd affectation for a PE teacher), he seemed to have the world sorted.

Edwards also was a new breed of football coach, and recognized something in Chris's rare skill, building our midfield engine room around Marsden's marvelous ability. He also saw something in me. Oftentimes he would scout out the other team's best attacker and counsel his midfielders to send some 50–50 balls to where I was marking the attacker. This was a time in British football when the game was far from beautiful. What do they say on American pick-up basketball courts? "No blood, no foul." I was a long way from being anyone's idea of a hard man, but I was a spirited, tenacious, and, at times, overzealous defender. Tackling in those days required you to make contact with the ball at some point during the assault on the opposing player, a task complicated by the often ankle-deep mud that passed as a pitch in the winter months. We were loyal to O.M., and he brought out the best of us as players, insisting we play constructive, pass-and-move football that ultimately brought trophies and acclaim to the school and to him as a coach and teacher.

Occasionally, he would stop by the Red Lion. My father treated him with deference, recognizing, I think, the high regard with which I held him. Under his influence, it became clear to me what I wanted to do with the rest of my life: I wanted to follow O.M.'s footsteps, and become a physical education teacher. As you age, you tend to look back on your life and reflect on those who have helped influence you in a positive manner, either through their actions, words, kindness, patience, or just being someone you want to emulate. O.M. Edwards was one of those people, someone who believed in me and my potential, and provided the opportunity and motivation for me to be the classic overachiever, exceeding my limited natural skills through sheer doggedness and will to win. I am forever in his debt.

◆

I remember those years as a blur of football, schoolwork, and long, grinding summer jobs. Work was my parents' life, a constant and unceasing component of their reality. We lived in Flintshire, one of the counties in Wales that had voted in 1961 to open pubs on Sundays, so it was a seven-days-a-week job, and Terry and Mal almost never took vacations.

There was a trip to the Isle of Man for the TT races—a vestige of the old days that survives even to this day—ludicrously dangerous motorbike time trials that invariably left someone dead or maimed. My father's attraction to the event was somewhat mysterious, in that he never drove a car, much less a motorcycle. But he took us all out there, and we sat amid the sunburned fans, surrounded by people drinking lager, playing bagpipes, or pointing to accidents at one part or another of the 37-mile course.

The only other continental family outing, taken in 1967, was a flight to Barcelona, and a long weekend spent in Calella, an out-of-the-way, down-on-its-luck resort outside of the city, with all of us cramped in a single room. That was also the trip, according to our retroactive calculations, during which my youngest sibling, my sister Emma, must have been conceived. Andy and Phil like to tell her that we were all there from the *very* beginning.

Longer, more frequent getaways were out of the question. Terry and Mal didn't trust anyone else to run the pub with the same dedication they did. So they worked. The forces that compelled them through a Depression and then World War II were beyond my understanding. As Pete Townshend wrote for the Who, "I've Known No War."

But some of that work ethic was inherited. From an early age, I had an intuitive willingness to work, and a striver's ambition. My first job at age 11 was as a "van lad" for Country Maid Bakery. I would get up at 4 a.m., get a lift to the bakery, and help load the crates of white and brown bread onto the van, then ride the route that occasionally went as far north as the Wirral, across the water from Liverpool. I would be rewarded with the princely sum of ten shillings—in my mind a king's ransom—to be saved and put toward a new pair of football boots for the upcoming season.

By 1967, still only 12, my father started trusting me to pull pints and mind the bar during the early evening shift at the Red Lion. It was unheard of, and certainly illegal. But no one complained. That was how I came to be a pre-teen publican, unbolting the door at 5:30, so Charlie Chippie and Wilf could take their place on their usual barstools, holding forth on the First Division, the latest village developments, and the unfathomable intricacies of Welsh politics. I would tend bar until 7:30 or 8:00, when my father would come downstairs for the evening rush.

By then, I had been watching my dad for so long, and had been part of the pub culture for so long, that I already knew how to pull a pint and mix a drink. To the regulars, I was a familiar face. But that was part-time work, and I recognized early on that to have the things I wanted to have and do the things I wanted to do, I needed a full-time job in the summer. This was where my father's vocation was a decided advantage. Among his regulars, there were any number of people who could set Terry's son up with a hard day's work and a decent paycheck.

After my years at Country Maid Bakery, I worked at Brymbo Steelworks for the British Steel Corporation, a union job that required me to simply sweep up and maintain the cleanliness of the premises. Going to work with the same purpose I'd done all my other jobs, I cleaned the entire area in 90 minutes. As I was finishing, one of the other workers walked over to my area and threw dirt down where I'd just cleaned. "You're working too fast," he groused at me. "This is your area. If they see you having completed the task too quickly, they're going to give us all more work to do, and we're going to have to work harder." It was a somewhat disillusioning experience, a realization that not everyone was as earnest as I was. It was not uncommon to open a utility closet at Brymbo and find someone literally sleeping on the job.

The next summer, I got a job working the night shift at Concrete Masonry, a local brick factory in Llay, the next village over. I'd ride my bicycle over to make it in time for the 10 p.m. to 6 a.m. shift, five days a week. (Every night before I left, my mum would pack me a massive sandwich, which we referred to as a "Scooby snack," as the *Scooby Doo* cartoon had by then worked its way across the Atlantic.) I'd work through the night in the brick kiln, where cement breeze blocks were being constructed in the massive oven. My job was to use large tongs to remove the 20-pound breeze blocks and then "cube" them—stacking the blocks on a pallet, then putting them on a hand truck to prepare for shipping. It was brutal work, but good money, and allowed me to afford my first car—a used green Hillman Imp—at the age of 16. It took three months of driving lessons, but I soon got my license and experienced a freedom that I'd never known before.

The summer of 1972 was even more involved, as I landed a job with Sir Alfred McAlpine, Ltd., one of Britain's largest public works contractors. I worked driving a water bowser along the construction of the mid-Wirral motorway, which would become the M53. My job was to drive the blocky, rusted Foden water truck, and water the path so as to keep the dust down, allowing the large Caterpillar scrapers following behind me to pave the route where the motorway was being built.

On the first day of the job, the foreman warned me to keep

my thumbs out of the steering wheel of the cumbersome truck, since it had no power steering. I nodded my head and instantly forgot about it, until a few hours into my first shift, when I hit a rock, and the steel steering wheel spun on me, breaking both of my thumbs. It was not a job for whiners; I went to the ER, had my thumbs set in a plaster cast, structured in a way that I could still grasp the steering wheel, and was back on the job the next day, humbled and very careful not to make the same mistake again.

The following summer I had a less bruising job, with the Arthur Monk Engineering firm. I worked as a surveyor's mate, on a major extension to the Stanlow Oil Refinery in Ellesmere Port, south of Liverpool, on the other side of the River Mersey. My job was to hold the leveling staff for the surveyor to view through his theodolite, to confirm his measurements and map out the terrain. There was none of the awful hours or constant back-breaking drudgery of the kiln, nor any of the dangerous, exhausting work of running the bowser. And yet I hated the job—the most boring work I've ever done in my life.

In sum, the summer work was good for me, and allowed me to have nice clothes and, eventually, a flash car. My brother Andy, only 13 months younger, was watching and admiring the results of the work, if not all of the work itself. In truth, Andy put in solid shifts at the Red Lion, but he didn't have the same consuming desire as I did. He did like my taste in clothes, though, and more than once nicked one of my shirts to wear for his nights on the town.

This led to a brawl that years later our younger brother Phil would refer to as Andy and my "alpha male fight." The specifics elude me, but I think what happened is that I found Andy had borrowed one of my shirts without asking, and perhaps ripped it during his carousing. It wasn't his first infraction, and I was less patient with Andy than I ought to have been—and he was likely less apologetic than he might have been. It prompted the only fistfight Andy and I ever had, but it was an epic brawl, starting on the lawn in front of the Red Lion, and progressing several hundred feet in various directions. In the midst of the swearing and shoving and grabbing, I took a wild swing at Andy, who turned his face away from the punch. Instead of connecting with his fleshy cheek, I landed a solid blow on his skull, and felt two of my knuckles shatter instantly.

The incident occurred only days before my all-important O levels in the spring of 1971, the crucial next winnowing process in the British school system. With my writing hand in a cast, I was reduced to having to answer the essay questions with the help of an amanuensis—a person who transcribed my verbal answers—who was retained by my family. It was a cumbersome and ultimately ineffective way to write essays. Besides raising my dad's ire over the cost ("Jesus Christ! What am I spending 50 pounds on?!"), it proved a futile effort and I didn't pass enough of the examinations.

I was at a crossroads, but confident that if I took the tests again after my hand had healed I would do fine. That meant me redoing my fifth form year. It was a humbling experience, but it came with an upside. The decision worked out well in every way it possibly could. I passed the O levels the next year and was able to attend Yale Sixth Form College, in the shadows of the Racecourse Ground, home of Wrexham AFC. This would be preparation for attending university, and also meant one more year of football under O.M. Edwards, and another year to play alongside my mate Chris.

Chris and I had played for a county all-star team of sorts, playing alongside Joey Jones (who'd go on to glory at Liverpool FC) and Mickey Thomas (who'd later star for Manchester United). We had more free time that final year as well, and Chris and I would often hang out with O.M. at his desk by the school gymnasium. We'd pepper him with questions. Occasionally, he'd go out and have drinks with us, and by that point he was playing in our Sunday League team—Marford FC, filled with several Yale High alumni players who were still in good shape—that excelled at the Brickie, a park with several football pitches.

But it was for Yale Sixth Form that we really excelled. The First XI had been a disappointment in past years, vying for the Ivor Tuck Trophy, the pinnacle for Welsh schoolboy sides. My last year at Yale, it all came together. Chris was at his best, a gifted athlete who was motivated by our coach. I had grown into one of the team leaders, holding down things at right back. We qualified for the final that year in South Wales and, by that point, we couldn't be stopped. We won 3–0 over a side from Duffryn, just outside of Newport in South Wales. Anointed the best school team in Wales, we celebrated on the three-hour drive back to Wrexham and stopped in at the Red Lion to toast our victory. No one did anything too crazy, but we did all get to enjoy a round on the house. Cheers, Dad!

Football and studies were my life at this stage. If I wasn't playing I would go to watch Wrexham at the Racecourse, or if I was really lucky, head up to Anfield to watch my Mighty Reds. In between I would study for my A levels, exams that I needed to pass to get to the next rung on the education ladder. I worked at the pub some in the summer of 1974, then prepared to go to university. Having passed my A levels, I'd been accepted at Madeley College of Physical Education, a wing college of Keele University.

By then, I'd done everything I wanted to do in Marford. Yale had won the Ivor Tuck Trophy. I had met my first girlfriend, Lynda, while working on the Country Maid route. We'd been going out for a while by the time I left for college, and we vowed eternal fidelity. I'd also worked enough at the pub and over the summers to afford a ridiculously flash car, a red 1971 Triumph GT6 Mark III. I'd already learned that the car doesn't make the man, and yet I've never been able to resist—once I had the means—buying the nicest car I could.

A wise man once told me that you should always have a car that, after you park it, you can't resist a glance back over your shoulder, and a smile, as you walk away. I'm still my father's son, but in this case, the father's son with wheels.

I was ready to go conquer the world, or at least the part of it that could be conquered by a physical education teacher.

CHAPTER FOUR

PHYSICAL EDUCATION

On an August morning in 1974, as business was opening for the day at the Red Lion, I hugged my mum and nodded a farewell to my dad. Then, carrying not much more than a duffel bag full of clothes and a sense of destiny, I climbed into my utterly unfit-for-purpose Triumph GT6 and set off forty miles to the east and Madeley College of Physical Education, nestled in the rural village of Cotes Heath, near Stoke-on-Trent, and not far from Stafford. I went to commence three years of university study that would enable me to realize what at the time seemed the outer limits of my life's desire—to be a physical education teacher just like O.M. Edwards, minus the pipe-smoking.

The Madeley freshmen were housed in the cramped quarters of Nelson Hall, which had all the charm—and many of the same architectural characteristics—of a military-style barracks. And for good reason ... it was built during World War II to house munitions workers toiling at the nearby Royal Ordnance factory. Forty students in a block, lined up in an H-shaped building, with each student in a small single room, with just enough space for a trunk at the foot of the bed and a small work table next to it. The design aesthetic was Mid-Century Gulag.

B Block was one of the four blocks for male physical education students. On the other side of the campus were several more blocks, inhabited by the women students, studying home economics, teaching, and science.

The British university system required physical education

students to prove their competence at both the physical and educational aspects of the job. We were in rigorous training on a daily basis, to both play and teach a variety of sports (over the course of three years, we were taught to master the teaching basics of something like 26 different sports; consequently, I could probably still recite the finer points of coaching badminton). But there was also extensive classroom work, centered around the sociology of sport as well as kinesiology, psychology, and multiple courses on biology and rehabilitative medicine, as a means to treat all manner of sports-related injuries.

The mixture was bracing. You'd come out of a long sports sociology class, and immediately have to dress out for a practical class, in which you'd have to learn the intricacies of, say, the pommel horse. I was no great shakes at gymnastics, but the muscle-bound rugby players struggled even more with the physical contortions necessary to master the apparatus. I actually feared for the equipment when the burly forwards were called upon to display their gymnastic prowess. Nearly everyone at the school was in excellent physical shape, and so the competition was honed to a fine edge. We would move from class to field and back to the class, sporting our royal blue tracksuits, emblazoned with the Madeley logo, a depiction of the Greek war hero Leonidas raising his spear. Looking back on it now, we were pretty full of ourselves.

There were the predictable hijinks and jackassery of a testosterone-fueled environment with that many young males. You dared not leave your dorm room unlocked or you might return from class one evening to discover that every article in your room had been relocated to the roof. One of my classmates woke up on his birthday to find that his friends had somehow moved his sports car into a fenced-in tennis court. There was so much joking, joshing, and outright bullshitting going on that we eventually had to devise a way to inform one another when we *weren't* joking. The password was "M.D.," which stood for "mother's death," a solemn vow on your mother's life that what you were saying was God's honest truth.

After exhausting days of study and physical activity, we would meet up at the campus pub, the Red Room, a humble enclave built a few years earlier to spare Madeley students the trouble of driving or otherwise navigating their way back to campus after a night of drinking. The Red Room had a linoleum floor, beer served in plastic glasses, and a bustling late-night service of cheese on toast, to take the edge off the excessively carbonated ale served there. Cramped and charmless, it still served its purpose. We'd gather and put a dozen or more chairs around a small table for drinking games. There was "Fizz/Buzz," a counting drinking game, where you had to say "fizz" on multiples of five and "buzz" on multiples of seven, with predictably poor results as the count went up. The most popular was the rhythmic drinking game "Names of Types of," in which each contestant would have to follow the lead of the first person in naming, say, a kind of car beginning with a particular letter—whomever broke the string had to drink.

After spending all day in their respective colleges, the Red Room was also the location for social interaction between the men and the women students. Between the hormones, the excess amounts of beer, and the barely monitored dorms, the joke was that on any given night a good number of the Madeley beds were empty, as students paired off and doubled up, usually in one of the ten women's dorms.

Moves were certainly being made there, but for the most part I wasn't one of the people making them. I was still pledging fidelity to my first girlfriend Lynda, who was also off at college, attending Bangor University. In retrospect, neither of us possessed the maturity or the skills necessary to maintain a long-distance relationship; in the event, ours came to a predictable end when Lynda and I went our separate ways.

I think back at the time now and realize that virtually all of the young men, myself included, were prone to bouts of unconscious sexism. Even among the most decent and mature of the eligible bachelors at Madeley, the attitude around the female students was more or less, "You're in the home-ec kitchen, we're running around the football pitch, we'll see you for a drink at night." Such was the cycle of daily life at Madeley.

I was living off a small stipend of £7 a month from my parents—enough for beer money at the Red Room—and calling home from a payphone every week or two, just to let them know I was still alive. I'd bring friends home for Christmas, and we'd often stick around long enough to watch Wrexham AFC play at the Racecourse on Boxing Day. Beyond that, I might swing back by Marford once or twice more during the school year, but mostly I was in my Madeley bubble.

Some periods in life stick with you, vivid in the memory, offering a new detail on a daily basis. Madeley was different. There was less time for solitude, less time for introspection, so the years were rendered somewhat indistinct, a cascade of physical activity, intense academic work, football and rugby matches against other schools on Wednesday afternoons and Saturdays, and—inevitably—drinking games nearly every night in the Red Room. My dominant mental image from those years is the feeling of sitting in a big circle, playing the "Names of Types of" drinking game in the Red Room, and waiting for my turn to name a piece of clothing that begins with S, with shirts, shoes, and socks long since named, then having the bloke in front of me shout "scarves" right when I was getting ready to say it next. That—or some variation of that—happened hundreds of times in the three years there.

◆

Arguably the two most prominent, compelling members of the Madeley faculty were lecturers who also doubled as coaches. One was Alan Hargreaves, a cerebral sort who ran the football program. Hargreaves—known simply as "H" to his players—was dignified and composed, a renaissance man who dabbled in arts and handicraft while harboring an academic's fascination with the sport (he would write instructional books about the nuanced strategy of the game). He was in charge of our first team, which was among the British university powers.

I played regularly during those years, usually at full back, though often moving to center half. My lack of speed was even more glaring at the college level, where my friend and teammate Dave Holland compared my turning radius to that of the *QE2*. But we enjoyed playing for H, and the games were a staple of Wednesday afternoons, with numerous pints of ale in the Red Room inevitably following every home match.

We played in the tournament for the British university championship under Hargreaves, but it was nothing like what I'd later see with college sports in the States. You could have two excellent amateur teams playing for a spot in the national tournament, but one has to remember that nearly every town of any size in Britain has its own football team somewhere in the English pyramid. So British intercollegiate sports followed the Corinthian model—in the deed the glory—and even for a big game, we'd have a crowd of just a dozen or so people, and one or two dogs in attendance.

At Madeley, I also grew devoted to the gregarious Edward "Eddie" Robinson, a charismatic carouser who ran the rugby program. I was no great shakes at rugby—I played for the third fifteen as a hooker—but enjoyed my time with the sport, save for the repeated instances when I got my face shoved in the grass in the scrum. And also the mornings after matches, when I had a preview of middle age, waking up to the sensation of every muscle in my body aching from the pounding. Somehow, Eddie made it all seem fun.

While Hargreaves was reserved and respectful, always strictly observing the dividing line between students and teacher, Robinson was decidedly less by-the-book, blurring that line frequently. Eddie was enthusiastic and collegial, often going out after matches to share a beer with his players. He was a remarkably engaging and persuasive person and would use those skills to maximum effectiveness in future years. He was already hustling for opportunities away from Madeley, sponsoring football clinics in the summers and networking with other camps around the UK and even in the United States.

◆

On Friday, January 31, 1976, the administrative staff at Madeley tracked me down on campus and told me I needed to call home at once. My dad answered the phone and told me a harrowing story: The previous night, a fire had started downstairs at the Red Lion—perhaps a burning ember that was never doused—that had engulfed the entire pub. Everyone was asleep upstairs when the heat from the fire began shattering windows downstairs. My brothers Andy and Phil were heroic, getting mum, dad, Nana Bree, and my sister Emma out my parents' bedroom window and onto the roof of the adjoining building. While Andy was shuttling the family to safety, Phil jumped down from the roof and ran across the street to call the fire department. Henry, our housecat, perished in the fire, and many of the family belongings were ruined, but everyone in the family survived.

I drove back to Marford that day to find two indelible sights. The first was our family home in ashes, all the furniture and fixtures in the pub destroyed, extensive smoke damage upstairs. But then there was the second thing: After twelve years in Marford, Terry and Mal Moore had become a bedrock part of the Marford community. And the community responded wholeheartedly. People brought meals—the kitchen was totaled—and clothes for the family. The regulars showed up at the usual time and started the renovation, moving the burnt furniture out to the slag heap. By 7 p.m. the next night, my dad was serving drinks amid the charred remains of the pub. There would be extensive renovations in the months ahead, and the Red Lion would be rebuilt, stronger and more modern than ever before. But the village of Marford's response in the wake of the tragedy exhibited the power of community at its very best.

Later that spring of '76, my dad got ahold of some tickets in the away end for Liverpool's regular-season finale against Wolves. By now, the team was Bob Paisley's, carrying on with the same vigilant excellence as Bill Shankly. Paisley was undoubtedly a less charismatic figure than Shankly, but he ran the team with perhaps more nous and a touch more sophistication.

Liverpool needed a win on the final day of the season at Molineux to win the league, and my dad and I went together (one of his friends drove). The Reds went down early, but then came back with three late goals. As the ref blew his whistle to signal the end of the season and the first league title in a decade, I joined most of the away end—though my dad hung back—in running out on the pitch in celebration. I found my favorite player of the era, Kevin Keegan, and patted him on the back of his No. 7 jersey. I remember thinking that it was a peak experience I'd remember the rest of my life, and the closest I would ever get to being an actual part of Liverpool Football Club.

◆

The final year at Madeley, 1976–77, found the stakes raised both academically and physically. The water was still not my friend. We had three sessions a week in the pool at Madeley, to learn how to earn our Royal Lifeboat Society Life Saving Certificate. I knew from early on that I was never going to be a water polo participant—swimming was challenging enough, much less having someone trying to hack you underwater anytime you had the ball in your hand.

But I progressed through the swimming requirements, preparing for the final test, in which we had to exhibit proficiency in all four swimming strokes. I had spent enough time in the pool at Madeley to become at least competent in the crawl, the breaststroke, and the backstroke. But the butterfly was completely beyond me. Not a natural swimmer to begin with, my body wouldn't cooperate with the rhythmic elevations that brought your nose above the surface of the water and allowed you to breathe. When the test came, I managed to desperately splash my way 25 meters across the pool doing some reasonable facsimile of a butterfly stroke. It was the closest to death I've ever come. I was hopeless, formless, but persistent. And I didn't drown. Little victories.

Those three wild, rambunctious, exhilarating years likely provided me with a solid foundation in leadership, communication, and the ability to motivate and mentor others—skills that are invaluable in any career. Training as a physical education teacher also strengthened my understanding of teamwork, discipline, and the physical and mental benefits of sport, which undoubtedly influenced my later career roles. Additionally, the experience cemented my lifelong love and respect for the benefits of sports and fitness, and for all of that, I am forever grateful to have been a "Madeley Man."

After graduation, I got a coaching gig in Stoke-on-Trent. One of the people Eddie Robinson had come across was a relentlessly optimistic American coach from Cleveland named Tom Hatfield, who brought a group of American high school students eager to learn the finer points of soccer, and I served as one of the coaches. It was the first glimpse of the growing interest in the game in America, where Pele coming out of retirement to play for the New York Cosmos had aroused the curiosity of millions of Americans, who were taking to the newly built American soccer pitches in record numbers.

In the summer of 1977, I began preparing for my first "real" job, as a physical education teacher at Ysgol Dinas Bran in Llangollen (Ysgol being Welsh for school). Though my teaching certificate would have allowed me to go anywhere in the UK, I wound up in a school about a half-hour's drive from the Red Lion.

It gave me an excuse to move back home. My parents had, earlier that year, purchased a new home in a development not 200 yards away from the front door of the Red Lion. They knew that someday they were going to retire, and when they did, they'd be forced to leave the premises. They'd fallen in love with Marford and wanted to stay close.

My father dubbed the house "Eurolea"—in honor of Liverpool winning both the European Cup and the league in 1977. But, consistent with his idiosyncratic nature and somewhat contrary attitude, he refused to set foot in the place until the day he finally quit the Red Lion—which was still another decade in the future. So I moved in, living rent-free but agreeing to pay all the utility bills.

That summer back home, I was struck by the changes in my family. My parents remained resolutely the same: dad was aging into a delightful curmudgeon, and my mum was the queen of the refurbished and improved kitchen. But Andy—by now seriously dating Chris Marsden's younger sister Sharon—was in love, and ready to venture out on his own. And my youngest brother Phil had, at age 15, already enlisted in the British Army. Mostly freed from the burden of their three sons, my mum and dad doted on the bright and bubbly Emma, and she reveled in the attention. Me and my brothers used to mutter to her that she got off easy; Terry and Mal had mellowed over the years.

My first day as a teacher was Wednesday, September 7, 1977. The following Saturday, three days into my professional career, I was at the Brickie, playing a game for Gresford Athletic in the Welsh National League against Lex XI, a club team from Wrexham. I had my usual pregame meal—a Mars chocolate bar about 45 minutes before kickoff. Ten minutes into the match, I went in for a 50/50 ball against Tony Davies, who'd been a classmate at Yale. To be fair, it might have been a 60/40 ball in Tony's favor, but with my usual bravado I charged in at full speed, blurring the thin line between brave and stupid. I stumbled a bit as I neared the ball, and Tony did the same, both of us slightly out of control, and as we came together, his knee pitched forward into my lower leg, and I can still hear the crunching sound of my tibia and fibula cracking from the contact. I knew instantly the leg was broken.

When they finally got me to Wrexham Maelor Hospital, the doctor asked me when I'd eaten last.

"I had a Mars bar about an hour and 15 minutes ago," I said.

He frowned and said, "Well, I can't give you a general anesthetic then."

So he had to reset the break by hand—among the most searingly painful things I've ever experienced—and then I was fitted with a toe-to-hip plaster cast.

That was bad, but even worse was having to make the difficult and embarrassing call to the Dinas Bran headmaster, Dan Jones, to explain that after three days of work, I had broken my leg and wouldn't be able to return for six to eight weeks, until I was out of the cast and able to move on crutches. Thankfully, and to my great relief, he was incredibly understanding and supportive.

I wound up back at the Red Lion, with my mum looking after me, and spent much of the next six weeks watching the BBC, and reading the six newspapers my dad got every day, as well as voraciously reading news magazines. I was never particularly good at just sitting around, and I didn't get any better during that fall.

When I finally got back to work that November, I found school mostly enjoyable. I commuted every day from Eurolea, now driving a more practical car—a Morris Marina coupe. It happened that the librarian at the school, a matronly woman named Mrs. Rose, lived just next door to the Red Lion, so I picked her up every morning for the 35-minute commute.

The interaction with the students was always energizing. It took me longer to connect with the other members of the faculty. I can remember sitting in the staff room, while history and English teachers would come in, wearing their tweed blazers and questionable ties, many speaking Welsh, and often looking down on the new guy in the tracksuit. But that was okay. I liked the kids, I liked the work, I liked my life, especially once the plaster cast came off and I could move again. Having said that, I always carried a chip on my shoulder as to how, as a physical education teacher, I was treated as part of the overall academic structure of the school. I was always eager to prove myself a capable addition to my fellow teachers in the classroom, but the closest I was allowed to get near a "real" subject was Social Studies ... a worthwhile pursuit, but lacking the prestige of History or English Literature. I was convinced I could have taught History or Geography, but "tracksuit lad" was restricted to his allotted swim lane and not allowed to venture near something requiring pen, paper, and homework. Social Studies was aimed at the fifth formers poised to leave school at 16 and pursue a profession "more fitting to their intellectual capabilities." That was code for obtaining an apprenticeship in plumbing, electrical fitting, or other worthy professions.

One moment in those classes has stayed with me all of these years, and was probably the trigger for me to start thinking about seeking a new profession myself. I've always had a pet peeve about double negatives, and mentally but silently correct people when I hear them. One of my students, Dai Gwyn Jones from Chirk, a town that was part of our school catchment area, was sitting in a front desk in one of my rare classroom sessions. After I gave the class a written assignment, Dai Gwyn, as rambunctious and disorganized as ever, threw his hand up, shouting "Sir, Sir, Mr. Moore—I ain't got no pencil, sir." In a valiant attempt to explain to him some semblance of correct grammar, I said, "Dai Gwyn!! Listen: *I* have no pencil." Spreading my arms wide, I proclaimed, "*THEY* have no pencil," then concluded with "*WE* have no pencil. Got it?" Convinced that I had made a breakthrough in his meagre command of the English language, I turned to the blackboard and began setting up the next assignment, only to hear him say under his breath to his best mate, Ryland Jones, "Well who the fuck has all of the pencils then?" It was at that moment I knew my teaching days were numbered.

I've always harbored some measure of shame as to how I handed out discipline to some of my more "anti-establishment" students, usually through the wielding of a size 11 Dunlop Green Flash plimsoll. It didn't come out of the locker very often, but there were times when I used it on the rear ends of selected troublemakers. For that I, to this very day, feel some level of guilt. Even though it was a different time and British society had a certain level of tolerance for corporal punishment, my heart really wasn't in it—there had to be a better way to keep those young lads in line.

Later in that fall of 1977, still on crutches, I got an international long-distance call at Eurolea, from the Clevelander Tom Hatfield, whom Eddie Robinson had introduced me to back at Madeley. He'd taken a shine to me at Stoke-on-Trent, and was calling to offer me a gig for the following summer.

He wanted me to come to the Cleveland suburb of North Olmsted, Ohio, and coach high school students there, along with running some clinics with the American Soccer League club the Cleveland Cobras.

A summer in the United States sounded like the most exotic prospect ever. I explained to Tom that I had a broken leg, but that I'd be fully recovered by next summer. We made a verbal agreement on the phone, and he promised he'd be in touch with an airline ticket and details. I didn't know it at the time, but that phone call would eventually change my career, the course of my life, and, eventually, even my nationality.

CHAPTER FIVE

THE NEW WORLD

In June 1978, I finished my first year teaching at Dinas Bran—it let out earlier than most schools, as the town of Llangollen would begin gearing up for the annual International Musical Eisteddfod, which brought choirs from all over Europe (and, eventually, the world) for a summer music festival. Just a few days later, me and my mates Brian Knowles and Mel Morris boarded a Laker Airways widebody L-1011 Tristar charter in London and flew to the United States, landing in Bangor, Maine, where the plane refueled and we went through customs. Then it was on to JFK in New York, where we caught a shuttle to Port Authority Bus Terminal. To this naive English lad, Port Authority seemed like the scariest place on earth, or at least the *weirdest*, like the cantina on Tatooine in *Star Wars*. From there we took a Greyhound bus to Cleveland. Our travel-weary group was greeted by Tom Hatfield, who would transport us to North Olmsted, where we'd spend the summer at the home of his friends Dick and Betty Bokanyi, boosters of youth soccer in the area.

Some people fall in love with America on the streets of New York City or in the casinos of Las Vegas or on the beaches of Miami. For me, the love affair began in suburban Cleveland, in the town of North Olmsted, where the Bokanyis and their three young children—Rick, Beth, and B.J.—lived in a farmhouse on five sprawling acres.

It was not just a new place; it was a new way of seeing the world, and moving through it. I had been transported from the rigid class system of the UK to something dramatically different, and from the cramped confines of British life to a lavish home with a large finished basement, a menagerie in the grounds, a garden, a swimming pool, three barns, and a stretch of woods in the backyard. Dick was a veterinarian, and it was clear from the animals on the property—there was a horse, a pig, rabbits, a sheep named Snowflake, ducks, chickens, dogs, any number of other critters—he loved his work.

I instantly felt welcomed by the Bokanyis, and was drawn to their warm cheerfulness. There were, of course, cultural differences to work through. But soon enough, me and my mates figured out that when one of the Bokanyis said *grodge* they meant garage, and in due course the Bokanyis figured out that when we said *gair-edge* we also meant garage. Beth would learn that when she said she was looking for her fanny pack, that sounded alarming to those of us from the UK. And we would learn that when we asked to be "knocked up" in the morning, that meant something entirely different in the States than it had back home. After that, everything else was easy.

Everywhere I turned in North Olmsted, there was a radical difference in size and volume compared to life in Britain. Bigger meals, bigger yards, bigger cars, and bigger garages, regardless of pronunciation. Everywhere there was plentitude; more choices in the supermarkets, more bathrooms in the home, even more refrigerators—the Bokanyis had one in the kitchen and another one in the garage for beer and soda, mostly beer. People were always coming over to the Bokanyis, or inviting them and us to their place for cookouts. For someone fascinated with pop culture, commerce, and conversation, coming to America was like a chocolate-lover getting dropped off at Willie Wonka's place.

The summer job, just down the street on the fields of the North Olmsted Soccer Organization, was both hard work and lots of fun. Hundreds of boys and girls were eager to learn the finer points of the game, and there was an armada of enthusiastic, well-intentioned parents eager to help. Cleveland, with its large ethnic population from eastern Europe, had long possessed a serious soccer infrastructure, and by 1978, even mainstream Americans were becoming soccer-curious. Tom Hatfield, who'd recruited me, was the Pied Piper of the enterprise, and what he lacked in knowledge of the nuances of the game he more than made up for in energy and enthusiasm.

Then there was an added advantage that we as Brits soon recognized. The mere fact of our British accents somehow conveyed to most Americans a level of sophistication and intelligence that we frankly did not possess. So we had come to a place we'd dreamed about, with seemingly endless abundance and optimism everywhere we turned, and people seemed abnormally interested in what we had to say simply because of the way we sounded when we said it. (I would later learn that this period in American history was described by then-President Jimmy Carter as registering "a national malaise." He should've spent some time in Great Britain—which had by then perfected a kind of baleful, knee-jerk pessimism about everything that made Carter's American malaise look like unrelenting sunshine to Brits like me.)

What I knew at the time was that Dick Bokanyi laughed more than any adult I'd known, seemed to have a bigger house than anybody I'd ever met who hadn't been born rich, and that there was nothing in Great Britain nearly as convenient or efficient as the Beverage Store, the drive-through liquor store that the Bokanyis used to frequent on their trips to replenish supplies. Sitting in the back seat, we'd look on in wonder as store clerks filled Dick's order and quickly brought two cases of beer out to the trunk—like an Indy pit crew for drinkers.

My mates and I were constantly in search of American experiences—bowling, amusement parks, miniature golf, drive-in theaters, shopping malls. Near the end of that first summer with the Bokanyis, Brian and I caught a Greyhound bus to California, where in Long Beach the Madeley professor Eddie Robinson was conducting clinics. We never saw Eddie that week, but we hung out with some of his proteges—friends of ours from the Madeley days—and then caught the Greyhound back to Cleveland in time for our return to the UK.

I promised Hatfield and the Bokanyis I'd be back, then I returned to Marford with all manner of American ephemera—T-shirts, stickers, toys. After the bracing summer reverie, I had come back to Britain at a time of economic stagnation, high unemployment, and pervasive social resentment best reflected in the burgeoning punk movement. I understood the resentment, and sympathized with the grievances, but I still didn't want to put a safety pin through my nose. Nor could I spike up my hair like the Sex Pistols, as I was already alarmingly follically challenged, with a hairline rapidly receding toward the back of my head. Not a great period in pop culture and fashion history to be going prematurely bald.

◆

By my second year teaching at Dinas Bran, I was growing comfortable with the job, and asserting myself to expand the program of offerings. Many of the students there were stocky farmboys, and they were mostly frustrated by the demands of stamina and flexibility required by football. I proposed introducing rugby to Dinas Bran—it was the national sport of Wales, after all. I eventually secured a grant for uniforms, and with some help from some of my younger colleagues, we got the teams at all age groups up and running—they were enthusiastic yet naïve, physical, but lacking in any finesse

I'd also figured out that what the kids needed most was

more exercise, so I inaugurated a series of lunchtime fun runs that soon had a healthy following, and an afterschool sports program. All this was met with tacit tolerance by my superior, a former gymnast named David "Dai" Price, who was a few years older than me, but firmly ensconced as the head of the physical education department at Dinas Bran.

One night, shortly after the fall 1978 term began, I went to the pub with two of my younger teaching buddies, Vaughn Williams and Nigel Parry. We found ourselves in nearby Gresford, and walked into one of our regular spots, the Griffin Inn, where we spotted a new, startlingly attractive woman behind the bar. She possessed the sort of head-turning beauty that would always get attention, and was wearing a man's shirt, unbuttoned to the point that guaranteed even *more* attention.

She was making a right bollocks of pulling a pint. I gallantly approached her and, employing my years of expertise, explained that she was doing it all wrong—she needed to tilt the glass, and rotate it so that she wasn't filling half the pint glass with foam. Accounts vary on what happened next; some would later say that I jumped over the bar to demonstrate, but I'm pretty sure I wasn't that bold or pompous.

It turned out she was bravely filling in as a favor to a friend, and after sharing my bartending tips, I engaged her in conversation when I could, and found her smart and outgoing, with a great laugh. I wasn't going to make an ass of myself by asking her on a date then and there, but somehow the subject of playing squash came up—the game was popular in the area back then—and I inquired if she would be up for a game sometime. She was amenable to that, so we set a time later that week to meet at the squash courts in Wrexham.

I confess I had no intention of actually playing squash. I never called to reserve a court, but instead showed up at the appointed time and explained to her that they were all booked, but since we were here anyway, would she fancy a drink?

Her name was Bernice Forward, and she had the can-do attitude to match her surname. Gorgeous, forthright, and intriguingly self-possessed, a fascinating mixture of self-confidence (she had a great figure and dressed to accentuate same) and British probity (she was very precise about language, cooking, and manners). She'd been a nurse in the British Army, a member of Queen Alexandra's Royal Nursing Corps, where she was elevated to sergeant. She worked the front counter at a chemist's in Gresford, and lived in a small house nearby, with an energetic, occasionally unhinged Irish setter named Dax, who seemed to require a daily half-marathon to work off his pent-up energy.

Bernice's father Cliff had been something of a legend in the area, a Royal Air Force veteran who made 548 appearances over twenty years for Wrexham's rugby club, serving as team captain and, after retirement, twice working as the club's chairman. Bernice was a teenager, one of four children when her mother passed; Cliff soon remarried and had four more kids, so by the time I met Bernice she was one of eight.

As we got to know each other, I learned she was going through a divorce from a member of the Scots Guards, and had recently been dating a guy. I won't say I swept Bernice off her feet, but I did start courting her and soon we were spending most of our free time together, often spending nights at her place or back at Eurolea.

She was a somewhat controversial prospect for my parents, who were not quite prepared for a girlfriend of mine showing up to the Red Lion in a leopard-print dress and ordering whiskey at the bar. But as we kept dating, they softened. Bernice was obviously bright, and also dependable. As our relationship deepened, Terry and Mal got on board, reasoning that if I was happy (and I was), then so were they.

◆

Teaching was fun, and I was enjoying my time with Bernice, but by the spring of 1979 I couldn't wait to get back to North Olmsted and America. The Bokanyis greeted me as if I were family—full of hugs and the sort of constant interest and encouragement I'd never received at home. We also had more sit-down dinners in any one of those summers than I'd had with my own family in my entire life. Let me be clear—it wasn't that I ever doubted my parents loved me; but by nationality and disposition, they simply weren't equipped to express that openly. The Bokanyis, like so many other Americans, were.

That second summer, we were joined by the thoughtful, genial Tim Booth, a grammar school friend of Brian Knowles from Nottingham, and a really skilled soccer player. He was as dazzled by the Bokanyis as I had been—Tim joked that his parents' car could fit in the trunk of the Bokanyis Caddy—and we bonded over what a refreshing departure the USA was.

That summer was another blur of sweltering days on the soccer pitches and glorious nights out and about. There were daylong adventures to Cedar Point, the massive amusement park which at that time had the world's largest roller-coaster. We would spend half the day riding the rickety Blue Streak, which looked like something you might see in a *Scooby Doo* episode. There were trips to the Great Northern Mall, where Tim and I would walk around wide-eyed at the bounty of goods for sale, and nights out at Pizza Hut, where I'd play Space Invaders with the Bokanyi kids.

Tim and I started making the rounds together that summer. There was a honky-tonk we frequented—the Cabin Club in Westlake—which featured some live music, mostly guitarists leading singalongs. We'd also hit a smaller place called Debbie D's out on nearby Lorain Road. Or else we'd wind up back near Cleveland Airport, at a bar in the Sheraton called the Final Approach, which offered a great view of both the airport and the city, a dance floor that was always full, and a bar that was always open.

I remember some discussions that summer with Tim, both of us speculating about how great it would be to come to America and live there. At the end of the summer, he was presented with an opportunity to stay, as the Cleveland State soccer coach Steve Parker offered him a scholarship. Tim took a while to deliberate, but eventually punched his American ticket, and came back the next summer for good.

At the end of my third summer with the Bokanyis, 1980, Bernice came out and visited North Olmsted, and she was intrigued by the American experience. Bernice and Beth would spend the days sunning in their pool, or shopping at the mall, and then we'd all go out drinking at night.

As the coaching work ended that summer, I was presented with a curious mission. Someone was moving from Cleveland to Benson, Arizona, and offered me $120 to drive the family car down there. It was a bulky Crown Victoria, with four tires bungee-corded to the roof. We had a week to get it down there, so decided to turn it into a proper road trip. The traveling party was Chris Marsden (who I'd convinced to join us that third summer), Mel Morris, Bernice, and me. We first went to Memphis, visiting Graceland and scarfing barbecue, then later crossed the endless expanse of Texas, and joined up with Route 66, staying in cheap motels along the way. When we reached Benson, we decided to head on out to the West Coast again, staying with a friend from Long Beach State who had been an exchange student at Madeley.

◆

After returning from another glorious summer in America in 1980, I began the third year of teaching with slightly less enthusiasm than before. Dai Price blocked any path I had for advancement at Dinas Bran, but there was something more nagging at me. My time in America had ignited a zest for life and a greater sense of self-belief and confidence. I can remember one class that fall, out with a group of schoolboys jogging along a path in the Welsh countryside and thinking, *Is this all there is? Running a group of schoolboys around the Welsh winter?*

It turned out the answer was no, but it was a while before I found that out.

The galvanizing event occurred on a dismal December day at Dinas Bran. Biting cold, snow slanting down nearly horizontal in the venomous Welsh wind. I was out teaching rugby to those brawny young farmers' lads, when one of the school secretaries shouted from the shelter of the door of the school: "Mr. Moore, you have a call from the United States."

I gave the students another drill to run, and hoped nobody would get hurt, and then hurried to the staff room. Amid the static on the line, it was my old Madeley professor Eddie Robinson, calling from California. He'd relocated there full time by then. Though our connection wasn't perfect, it was clear that he was offering me a job—his start-up Action Youth America needed a director of soccer, and he wanted me to move to the States permanently, helping him coach in Long Beach and joining him in the land of summer beaches, bikinis, and, rather regrettably, Speedos.

At that moment, time seemed to slow down and I became acutely aware of the gravity of the moment. I noticed the telephone in my right hand, saw the cord dangling down by my tracksuit bottoms. I looked out the frosted window to see the snow pelting the dim, late-afternoon Welsh countryside, and it occurred to me that whatever was waiting for me in California had to be better than this.

"Eddie, let me think about it," I said. "I'll get back to you."

My parents were easy. They didn't presume to know better. Mal and Terry weren't the sort to question the advisability of quitting a good job with benefits, or to suggest that I write down all the pros and cons in two separate columns on a piece of paper. Bernice didn't take much convincing, either, and made it clear that she was willing to come along.

Robinson had always been very persuasive, but in this instance I didn't take much persuasion. I had no chance to advance at Dinas Bran, with Dai Price being a "blocker" on my career ladder, and I was too young to give up the prospect of adventure. I already knew I loved the United States, and if I didn't jump at the opportunity now, the chance might never come around again.

I accepted the job and made arrangements to come out in the summer of 1981. Late that spring, all of our friends and family came to a send-off at the Wrexham Rugby Club—Cliff Forward was of course still a member—and we sang and danced and drank, and prepared to go out in pursuit of our American dream.

It was a leap of faith that, like a lot of immigrant stories in the USA, would get off to an extremely bumpy start.

CHAPTER SIX

AMERICAN LAND

The first thing you must understand about Eddie Robinson is that he was equal parts rainmaker and instigator, a moveable feast with a consummate skill for persuasion. With a Geordie lilt in his voice and a gleam in his eye, he could talk almost anyone into almost anything. When he'd offered me the job in Long Beach, he had been bristling with enthusiasm but rather sparing with the details.

He explained that he had set up his Action Youth America soccer program at Veterans Memorial Stadium, where California State University, Long Beach had played their football games up until 1977, when they moved to the Big A in Anaheim. As we embarked on our great American adventure, Bernice and I knew we were going to be in California, and I knew I'd be working and conducting camps at Veterans Memorial Stadium. Eddie had neglected to mention that we'd all also be *living* in the stadium. He had purchased three dilapidated old mobile-home trailers on the site, none with running water, and they were set up around the edge of the field. He lived in one, the bright fellow Madeley grad Dave Telling (the amiable Brit who actually looked the part of a California surf dude) would eventually be in another, and Bernice and I would be in the third. Eddie also conveniently hadn't informed me, until the day I arrived, that I needed to immediately enroll at California State University, Long Beach, and start working toward my master's degree, so I could remain legally in the States on a J-1 student visa.

Eddie, God bless him, had sold me a classic bait and

switch. I went for it because I desperately wanted to come to America. He probably could have sold me beachfront property in Oklahoma, and to be clear, despite the lack of details accompanying the opportunity, I am forever in his debt for providing me with a gateway to what I had hoped was The American Dream.

I had arrived a week or so ahead of Bernice, and prepared myself for her reaction to our new home. Anyone who's had a romantic partner knows the feeling of mortification when an idea you've pitched and sold turns out to be less than advertised. But this wasn't like I'd dragged Bernice to a bad movie or a disappointing concert. I'd sold her on a vision of American prosperity based largely on my time with the Bokanyis in North Olmsted, Ohio—except with California sunshine and beaches. However, she was suddenly thrust into a situation in which almost every action—making coffee, cooking a meal, taking a shower, or using the bathroom—was a chore. I was up for it, ready to be all in to realize my American Dream. She was, shall we say, less pleased. To her credit, she didn't turn on her heels and return to the airport and buy a ticket back to Wales (although that may have been because neither of us could have afforded a return ticket at that point). But we were living in America, pursuing our dreams, playing the long game, and that would override the initial less than optimal living conditions. So we hoped...

I recognized the challenge and did what I knew: I went to work. The precious commodity that Eddie had was the stadium itself. It was owned by the city, and the football team's decision to vacate had created an opportunity which Eddie seized upon. The stadium shared a parking lot with a mammoth McDonnell Douglas plant, where they were building the MD-80s. The company then had hundreds of immigrant engineers and technicians, many of whom wanted their growing families to have exposure to the world's game. As soccer continued its slow incursion in the States, there was a growing cadre of youths who were going out for the sport.

We also tapped into a burgeoning adult soccer scene. Among the people I regularly dealt with at the Long Beach Youth Soccer Organization were Gordon Rule, a Liverpudlian expat who'd settled in Long Beach as a longshoreman, and worked himself up to the managerial level, and an American named John Albertson, who was a Miller Beer operations manager. They both possessed distinctly American can-do attitudes, such that the vague ideas we would hatch over beers at the Thirsty Isle tavern (home of the 34 oz. "Schooner" beer, for those who like to buy in bulk) would somehow come to fruition. One night, several beers in, we decided we wanted to open our own soccer shoe and equipment store—Soccer City—which we eventually got up and running, largely staffed by Gordon's five children (one of whom, Sharon, also worked as Eddie's secretary and later married Dave Telling). Gordon and John also helped me put together the Southern California Professional Soccer League, an adult weekend league with 12 teams, many with a heavy ethnic orientation. Artesia DES was full of Portuguese, the Garden Grove Galactica was full of Eastern Europeans, Cerritos Holland was led by Dutch players. I wound up as player/coach for our team, the Long Beach Tornadoes, which included a decent British contingent with some locals mixed in.

We probably should have called it the Southern California (Barely) Professional Soccer League, but we'd sell tickets and draw a few hundred fans to Veterans Stadium. It was fun, and Eddie and I began promoting these local soccer games on Saturday evenings and local rugby matches on Sunday.

We'd sell beer at the concession stands for the game, but then we went a step further. We completely renovated a room under the stands, turning it into a reasonable facsimile of an English pub. We borrowed a camcorder to film the games, and then had a TV monitor and a VCR in the pub. After we'd shoot footage of the games, we'd invite the tired, sweaty players to the pub with their girlfriends, to buy dollar beers and experience the ego gratification of watching their games replayed on video.

Saturday nights were a chore; after everyone left, around 9 or 10 p.m., Eddie and Dave and I would spend hours reconfiguring the field for rugby—moving the goals, taking down the corner flags and redrawing the field lines for rugby, then cleaning the pub for the ruggers to come in on Sunday.

During the day, I helped Eddie bring whatever commerce we could into the stadium. We still shared the property for certain events—Long Beach Poly high school football games inside the stadium, carnivals and swap meets in the massive parking lot—but mostly it was our domain. Every weekday, I'd set out in a bus on a circuit of local schools in and around Long Beach, picking up kids in the area who'd signed up for our after-school program.

I don't remember what my salary was, but it was embarrassingly low—maybe $200 or $300 a week. (Dave Telling came on at $5 an hour, so I wasn't complaining.) For all the challenges, the Long Beach soccer community was extraordinarily welcoming. An expat loaned me the temporary use of an old Ford Galaxy to drive around town for a while, and I later spent $800 on an old green Datsun B210. Beyond that, I was doing anything I could to make ends meet. I led concentrated small-group training with students after school, at $4 a head. Later, I drove around the area giving clinics to aspiring coaches, working on their initial coaching licenses. When I wasn't working during the day, I was attending classes at night, and spending any spare money I had on tuition. This was a classic immigrant story of doing whatever you could to keep your head above water until you could form a solid platform for your family from which they could springboard into their own lives as first-generation Americans.

Money was impossibly tight, but Bernice and I discovered the wonder of happy hour, a concept for which there was, at that time, no British analog. We'd go to a place like the Thirsty Isle or the delightfully old-school Joe Jost's (a Long Beach institution since the '20s), home of pickled eggs. At some of these taverns, a free buffet of chicken wings came included with the drinking. We became connoisseurs of bargain food, of all-you-can-eat buffets, and the Grand Slam Breakfast at Denny's, or a Mexican restaurant called El Torito—our first experience with the free appetizer of chips and salsa.

The stadium operation was just starting to generate some momentum when one day Henry Zimmerman, a representative from Long Beach City, stopped by to check in. Surveying the operation, he asked Eddie how he was possibly making any money.

Eddie smiled ruefully and said, "The beer, mostly."

"The beer?," asked Henry. "What does the A.B.C. have to say about that?"

"Who's the A.B.C.?," Eddie asked.

"Oh, fuck!" said Henry, eyes widening. "You guys are in the shit."

Zimmerman had realized in an instant that Eddie had not cleared alcohol sales with California's authoritarian Alcohol and Beverage Commission. The beer sales soon dried up, and not long after, Eddie's sketchy financial model began to fall apart. I knew he couldn't afford to keep us and it was just as well, because we couldn't afford to stay. Everything was good-natured, but the business model (it was more of a business *notion*, really) wasn't sustainable. By the fall of 1982, Bernice found out she was pregnant and I realized that if we wanted to stay in the States—and I very much did—I needed a real job.

◆

In addition to my director of soccer role with Action Youth America, I had been working as an "Ekin" (Nike spelled backwards), a field reporter for the nascent Beaverton, Oregon shoe company Nike, which had reps all around the country, reporting on sales trends and consumer attitudes, in exchange for a credit on Nike shoes and athletic gear.

I'd heard through the athletic shoe grapevine that the French company Patrick was looking for a regional salesman. The company was one of the many independent operations that had grown to an international presence. Patrice Bénéteau, the son of a shoemaker in the French town of Pauzauges in the French Vendée, began making athletic shoes in 1929, for soccer, rugby, cycling, tennis, squash, even badminton. By 1979, Patrick was a prestigious name, and had signed my Liverpool hero Kevin Keegan (who'd gone on to Germany to play for Hamburger SV) to an endorsement deal. The Keegan Gold model, crafted out of kangaroo skin, was a big seller, as was the Platini Super, endorsed by French superstar Michel Platini

I drove up to San Rafael, California, just north of San Francisco, for the interview. By then, I think I was already good at pitching myself. I got the offer and I jumped at it. The attractions of the job were the use of a company car—a new Toyota Camry, to replace the Datsun—and a monthly draw against commission of $2,000.

The soccer shoe market in America at the time featured a broad assortment of competitors. The German brand Adidas had the lead, but there were other brands—Nike, Puma, the growing presence of Umbro, Lotto, Diadora, and smaller companies fighting for their share of the soccer market.

My job was essentially that of a door-to-door salesman, but I had a built-in advantage. I already liked Patrick shoes, and I could speak knowledgeably about why they were good. Armed with nothing more than a trunk full of shoe samples, a notebook of order forms, and a Thomas street guide to Los

Angeles, Orange, and San Diego counties, I began combing the area and pitching every store that might sell soccer shoes. I started with about a hundred accounts, mostly big chains. But I was convinced we could do more by reaching out to the soccer specialty stores, the independents popping up all around the area.

I was cold-calling virtually every sporting goods shop in southern California, going as far south as San Diego and as far north as Santa Barbara. I'd drive into a town, go to a payphone, inspect the Yellow Pages, then tear out the page or pages listing the sporting goods dealers. Then I'd use my Thomas guide to get to as many different stores as I could. "Hello, I'm Peter Moore," I'd say, laying on the accent as thick as I could while still remaining intelligible to American ears. "I am the local rep for Patrick, the French soccer shoe company. I wonder if the owner or buyer is available, please. I've got my samples in the car if he or she has the time. I'd like to take them through the collection and show them how good this line of shoes is."

If I could see them then, I would. Otherwise, if I could get an appointment, I'd come back the next week and give them the full 90-minute presentation. In most cases, if they didn't know soccer, I earned their trust. The buyers who did know soccer were even easier—often they were dying to talk with anyone who knew and loved the game as they did. With some of them, I could even say "football boots" rather than "soccer cleats," reverting to my native language of all things football. Over the next decade, I'm sure I gave a thousand of those 90-minute presentations. Patrick's greatest asset was a comfortable, quality shoe associated with top names—Keegan and Platini—well-known in soccer circles. My greatest assets were my work ethic and, still, my British accent.

◆

As I was starting work at Patrick, I knew I wanted to immerse myself in the culture of my new home, to venture out and meet a wider cross-section of Americans. There had been a close-knit cohort of British immigrants in the Long Beach soccer scene and I felt comfortable among them, but for the most part they stayed among themselves. I knew I wanted to branch out, to become more familiar with American culture, cuisine, and customs. It was in Long Beach that I ate pizza for the first time, and after a lifetime of the inevitable British salad cream on salads, I was suddenly exposed to the myriad of salad-dressing options in the States. I still remember tasting Thousand Island dressing for the first time, and wondering, *My God! Where has this been all my life?!*

I also strove to better understand the American institutions of baseball and football. If I was making the rounds of shoe stores on a Wednesday, and the Dodgers were home, I'd go by Chavez Ravine and get discounted tickets. One Dollar Wednesdays! Invariably, I'd sit next to someone who was more than happy to explain the nuances of the game to me. Eventually, I stumbled onto the greatness of the Dodgers' radio play-by-play man, Vin Scully, and his elegant and precise commentary became part of my southern California soundtrack, along with the two powerhouse rock stations in LA, KROQ ("K-Rock") and KRTH ("K-Earth"). In the fall, I'd follow the Los Angeles Rams, by then playing their games in nearby Anaheim.

After we found out Bernice was pregnant, we moved to a small apartment and decided to get married. There was neither the time nor the money for a proper wedding back home, so in December 1982 we got married on the *Queen Mary*, which had been purchased by the city of Long Beach and docked in Long Beach Harbor in 1967, after more than a thousand crossings of the North Atlantic. None of our family was there, so it was a casual affair, consisting entirely of our new California friends. I do recall a spirited reception, at Sam's Seafood in Huntington Beach, right on the PCH, with Dave Telling playing guitar and singing with his band the Cast of Few, serenading us with covers from the Police and other contemporary hits.

Bernice and I had no money for a proper honeymoon, though we did get back to Cleveland to see the Bokanyis. Bernice was still in the States on just a travel visa, and we agreed it made more sense for her to return to Britain and have the baby there.

On May 3, 1983, I received a call from a friend from the Red Lion who worked at the GPO—the General Post Office in Britain, which ran both the postal and telephone system in the UK. "Peter, congratulations—you have a healthy daughter," he said, and we soon rang off. I felt a sense of awesome responsibility, and knew my life had changed in that instant. After Bernice returned with baby Tara, I grew to love the joys of fatherhood and the rapid development of our bright, watchful daughter.

In those coming years, Bernice and I fell almost too well into our respective roles. I was desperate to succeed and provide for my growing family, pouring myself into work, traveling all around the region, almost always on the move. Bernice threw herself into the raising of Tara, and also took on more work as a nanny, first with a boy named Matthew, a child of our neighbors Carol and Gary White, and later with triplet babies, working for the Boucher family in Huntington Harbor. She was ever the nurturing nurse, dedicating her life and her own considerable intelligence to the children.

Our natural personalities were further emphasized. Always outgoing, I became more so, realizing that I could leverage my accent, my drive, and my personality to succeed—the Patrick sales in my region went up 300 percent in the space of two years. Always reserved, Bernice became more so, more careful, more cautious, more protective of our child and the other children in her care.

◆

All the while I was working, the industry was changing. The harbinger was the 1984 Los Angeles Olympics. I went to events every day, occasionally as a rep of Patrick, but many times simply as a fan. For all I knew, it would be my one and only chance to attend an Olympic Games. After the dismal financial losses suffered by the 1976 Olympic Games host Montreal and the Western boycott of the Moscow Olympics (in protest of the Soviet Union's invasion of Afghanistan), Peter Ueberroth and the LA Olympic Organizing Committee made some ingenious changes in the way the Games were run. Instead of the riot of hundreds of small sponsorship deals, the LAOOC offered a limited and highly exclusive set of sponsorships to several key groups—scarcity was a strength. Despite the Soviet boycott, the Games were a commercial and sporting success. Ticket sales and TV ratings were great, and it was the greatest fortnight of traffic in the modern history of LA, as almost all of the locals—fearing the worst kind of tourist logjams—stayed in. I flew down the usually clogged freeways, seeing more accounts in a single week then I could ever have managed in "normal" traffic conditions.

Later that year, I was promoted to regional sales manager, and we moved to northern California. We found a home in Rohnert Park, in Sonoma County, while my new office was the Patrick USA headquarters in San Rafael. It was a massive change for me. I went from working for myself—each day with the Thomas guide and samples in my trunk—into an executive role, suddenly overseeing a team of 42 sales people. I realized quickly that I needed to use the same powers of persuasion that I had been using with store-owners and buyers to now influence my own sales team, many of whom were reps for multiple companies.

And here a maxim from the late Southwest Airlines founder Herb Kelleher comes to mind; he noted that most companies say the customer comes first. Kelleher changed the paradigm—at Southwest, he said, the *employees* come first, reasoning that if the employees felt valued and respected, they would in turn treat customers the same way. So it was at Patrick, where we held sales retreats in the wine country, and tried to cajole, inspire, and support the sales force in any way we could. Patrick remained a niche brand, but one in a position of strength in its quality and European heritage. The brand enjoyed a small but loyal following in the States. With my help, it was growing.

I was learning on the job, quickly I hoped. My work had been transactional, but now I had to be strategic. I had never taken a business class, but I was soon confronted with needing to learn all the skills taught in those classes: forecasting the future, finding the best way to allocate limited resources, being responsive and vigilant without becoming a micromanager. Making one more call or writing one more memo at the end of a long day.

Along the way, I did more of what I'd done growing up at the Red Lion: a lot of watching and a lot of listening, becoming a student of human nature. By the time I got to San Rafael, I knew the market cold—knew what price points worked best, what range of shoe sizes to offer depending on the clientele in the area (heavy immigrant populations with Eastern Europeans tended to skew toward bigger shoe sizes, Mexican-American communities often skewed smaller).

The move to northern California and Patrick's American home office in San Rafael also put me in close quarters with the combustible, iconoclastic president of Patrick USA, Peter Strauli. He was a Swiss who'd emigrated to the US, and was working for the French athletic footwear company despite quite obviously despising the French. A chain-smoking heavy drinker, Peter was a man of prodigious ego and appetites, and was on his seventh marriage when I met him.

Patrick's San Rafael headquarters was in the Canal District, a well-worn, rundown part of the city. Outside of the office, it was not uncommon to encounter hypodermic needles or used condoms on the street. While breathing in the secondhand smoke of Strauli, I was trying to figure out a way to raise Patrick's profile, while having only a fraction of the advertising and endorsement budget of the main players like Adidas, Nike, and Puma.

I'd come in during the early stages of a movement that was changing both athletic footwear and culture as a whole. You might call it the Great Casualization of America, and though the change in footwear was only one part of a larger trend, it signaled a broader shift. In many offices, it was becoming pointless to show up in a suit and tie every single workday. It became apparent with the growing sales of Patrick's new indoor soccer shoe—the sporty black Stabil—that the clientele went beyond people buying the shoes for indoor soccer. Athletic footwear was becoming a fashion industry.

We'd seen Chuck Taylors cross over into the early days of punk, and the Adidas Stan Smith worn well after the tennis matches were over, but this was something new, and at a different order of magnitude. People were wearing the Nike Cortez and Adidas Sambas at dance clubs and in movies. By the early '90s, Run-DMC was rapping about "My Adidas" and Whitney Houston was rocking a pair of Nike Cortez for her performance of the national anthem before Super Bowl XXV.

◆

Throughout the decade of the '80s, I followed Liverpool FC as best as I could from afar, but I saw virtually nothing. None of the papers I read—the *Long Beach Press Telegram* or the *Los Angeles Times*—could be relied upon even to print final scores, much less game stories. I would often go to a payphone on Sunday morning, and armed with a batch of quarters, call my father for a short update. He wouldn't have seen the match, either, but he provided details. Gordon Rule's family back in Liverpool would send copies of the *Liverpool Echo* Saturday Pink, so we would read those two weeks after the fact. Even at a distance, we took pride in the team's triumphs—Liverpool won six league titles during the '80s, and two European Cups (later renamed the Champions League), two FA Cups, and four League Cups.

But it was clear that Americans had a skewed vision of the sport. When news about soccer did make it over, it was usually bad news, such as reports of the Heysel disaster in 1985, in which 39 Juventus fans died after an encounter with Liverpool supporters in a stadium not fit to host a European final. That tragedy caused English clubs to be banned from international competition, and perpetuated the myth that all supporters were lawless thugs.

That was an awful time, and on April 15, 1989, it got worse. I was representing Patrick, talking to a sporting goods dealer in El Paso, Texas, when we heard the first radio reports of trouble at Hillsborough, where Liverpool were facing Nottingham Forest in the FA Cup. Later that day, when grainy pictures showing the panic and disarray at the stadium led the nightly news, my blood ran cold, thinking of the repercussions if Liverpool fans were once again seen as culpable.

It was one of the darkest days in the history of football and in the history of Liverpool, as nearly a hundred of the Liverpool fans who went to that match never came home. They lost their lives due to the gross negligence of the South Yorkshire Police Department, and there was a subsequent cover-up—backed by the despicable Fleet Street tabloid *The Sun*, which baselessly perpetuated the lies that drunken, late-arriving supporters were responsible. This official account stood for nearly three decades, before it was finally corrected after a second inquiry. In 2016, then British prime minister David Cameron issued an official apology and admitted, "All families and survivors now have official confirmation of what they always knew was the case, that the Liverpool fans were utterly blameless in the disaster that unfolded at Hillsborough."

At the time, though, all I knew was that the people had died, and Liverpool supporters were being blamed for it.

◆

By then, my life and job had changed again. Our son Tyler was born in 1986, making my and Bernice's lives at once all the more rewarding and all the more challenging. Two years later, Patrick was purchased by a Belgian consortium. They sent auditors around to each of their regional offices, and they were not happy with the way that Strauli was running the business. One day in 1988, we were informed Strauli was out. Not long after that, I was promoted to president of Patrick USA—less than six years after selling shoes out of the trunk of my trusty Camry, I was now the president of the company. This gave me the freedom to move the offices out of the dodgy section of San Rafael and into Rohnert Park, closer to where we were living.

The job had grown more challenging in the meantime. By the late '80s, two factors were transforming the athletic shoe industry. The first was the rise of Nike, and its winning bet on basketball superstar Michael Jordan. The Spike Lee-directed commercials featuring the Air Jordan raised the stakes of competition to an entirely different level. Meanwhile, the British/American company Reebok was experiencing astounding growth in the female athletic shoe market, jumping on the aerobics craze.

Patrick was on a positive run with the Stabil Noir, as well as the Platini Super and the Keegan Tactic. But we were, in a marketing sense, bringing a knife to a gunfight. We would go to the big European sporting goods convention, ISPO Munich, or the big American confab, the Super Show in Atlanta, with Patrick stickers or T-shirts for our best clients. Meanwhile, the big four companies—Adidas, Nike, Reebok, and Puma—were outspending us exponentially. Nike was bringing the Temptations into their giant exhibition space for concerts.

In 1991, our third child, Toni-Marie was born. We had a wonderful home in a cul-de-sac in Rohnert Park, we were scouting out schools, and we were becoming comfortable in our milieu. But even then, I recognized that in the new world order of the Sports Shoe Wars, small companies like Patrick would have trouble competing.

In late 1991, with all of this weighing on my mind, I got another phone call that would change my life.

CHAPTER SEVEN

SNEAKER WARS

I'd been at Patrick for about a decade when I received a call late in 1991 from a recruiter for Reebok, at the time one of the largest athletic footwear companies in the world. The offer that followed—to become the company's first director of football—felt very much like being called up to the Major Leagues. I was tabbed at the behest of one of the legends in the business, the flamboyant Uruguayan Roberto Muller, who'd conceived and built the Pony brand in the '70s, relying on the image and star power of athletes long before anyone had heard of Michael Jordan. Under Muller, Pony located the intersection of athletic performance and hip leisurewear, recruiting the likes of Pele, Earl Campbell, Reggie Jackson, and others to wear the shoes with the distinctive Pony "chevron" on the side. I had gotten to know Muller casually on the Soccer Industry Council of America (SICA), where he was one of a handful of internationals who truly understood the game, and what it would take to import it to America.

By the late '80s, Muller had sold his stake in Pony and was being recruited by Reebok's chairman and CEO, the Boston-based executive Paul Fireman, the entrepreneur who'd begun his career selling camping equipment and fishing tackle before meeting Reebok's British founder at a sporting goods show in 1979, and acquiring the rights to be the company's American distributor. Within five years, Fireman had bought the company outright and revolutionized the industry, with the introduction of the first aerobics shoe—the Freestyle—with softer leather and a wider palette of colors.

Suddenly, women by the millions across the country were buying athletic footwear, and Reebok was selling most of them.

Fireman finally coaxed Muller aboard in 1990, with a mission to expand Reebok's global reach. Like Roberto, I was brought in to solve a problem created by the company's success. Though Reebok was growing in market share, elbowing in among the heavyweights like Adidas and Nike, the company continued to make most of those gains in the women's market. At Reebok's headquarters in Stoughton, Massachusetts, 20 miles south of Boston, it was clear the brand needed to make inroads with men, and that meant having a greater presence in the soccer business, both domestically and abroad.

Bernice and I discussed the opportunity at length, and decided that the transformation—West Coast to East Coast, president of a small company to the director of a much larger company's new division—was a risk worth taking. I left in January of 1992, while Bernice and the kids waited until the end of the school year to join me. We eventually settled in a beautiful home in Medfield, about a 25-minute drive from Reebok's headquarters.

◆

Muller was fascinating to work with, a man constantly in motion, at once full of energy and bluster. His m.o. was a constant stream of ideas, some of them legitimately brilliant and some of them completely ludicrous. If you worked for Roberto, you learned to listen carefully, always remaining mindful of discernment, and to redirect him when he started going off on an impractical tangent. But mostly I was left to my own devices. As president of the company, Roberto was dealing with dozens of global issues across all platforms, handing off to me the task of Reebok's arrival on the soccer scene.

It was as though I'd been driving an old clunker for years, and was suddenly put behind the wheel of a high-performance sports car. Reebok's advertising and marketing budget for a month far outpaced what Patrick would spend in a year. And as soon as I arrived in Stoughton, I realized the company had talent to burn. I assembled a team of forward-thinking, hard-working and hard-headed innovators. Christian Tresser was the designer (who'd already experienced success with his debut at Reebok, the introduction of the Aztrek running shoe), Andy Tate the engineer who would bring form to Tresser's visions, and John McCluskey the marketing man—the consummate hustler and an American who had an affinity for the game, and would make sure the rest of the footwear world was paying attention. The ultimate goal was to get Reebok's distinctive but somewhat unwieldy and aesthetically complicated "vector" logo as recognizable as Nike's swoosh or the three stripes of Adidas.

We knew we had to expand all of Reebok's soccer offerings—the full gamut of gear from uniforms to balls to the training range—but it all would start with the shoe. Going against the growing industry trend of sourcing from factories in Asia, Reebok found a shoemaker in Italy that could handle our ambitious production schedule. We piqued interest in 1993 with a Leo Burnett teaser ad campaign that included full-page ads in *Soccer America* and other magazines, reading simply, "If you dribble... get ready to drool."

When the Reebok Integrity Pro finally rolled out, accompanied by endorsements from Ryan Giggs, Denis Bergkamp, and Andy Cole ("The Boot on the Deadliest Foot in Britain"), it was clear that we were going to make some headway. We'd make further gains later with the Sidewinder, as Tresser's eclectic sensibilities opened up the field of elite soccer boots, which in the past had been limited largely to black leather with big white logos.

We were still establishing ourselves when the World Cup came to the United States in 1994. I remember that summer well, both for its successes (every ticket to every game sold out, a first in World Cup history) and its failures (putting natural grass into indoor stadiums had a punishing greenhouse effect, and watching soccer players try to toil in the sweatshop of the Pontiac Silverdome was a reminder why soccer was meant to be played outside).

In trying to announce our presence, the objective was simple—to get as many players as possible to wear Reeboks. The world's biggest stars were almost all on four-year contracts with various companies, but most players on most national teams were unaffiliated, and willing to negotiate. Quality shoes were necessary of course, but to clinch the deal you needed cash. A player from South Korea or Cameroon could be persuaded to wear Reeboks in exchange for an endorsement fee. But you weren't going to get people to fill out tax receipts or give you their checking account routing numbers. The coin of the realm, as with so many things in the world of FIFA, was American dollars. So for USA '94, McCluskey and I greeted as many teams and players as we could, and the going rate for starters who weren't under contract was $1,000 per game. We provided the shoes before the game, and made sure the players wore them (McCluskey had a team of Reebok employees monitoring all the games, and a spreadsheet keeping track of the dozens of different players we'd struck deals with). Then afterward each player would stop by and pick up an envelope with $1,000 in twenties.

I'd pushed hard to get Brazil to sign a kit deal with Reebok, but had to "settle" for Argentina when the *Seleçao* signed with Nike. That year, I spent an inordinate amount of time in Buenos Aires getting the deal done with the Argentinian

Federation and its rather slippery president Julio Grondona, who was also a senior vice-president at FIFA, and later implicated in the bribery and corruption scandals surfaced by the US Department of Justice. Though we hadn't gotten the deal with Brazil, we did have the satisfaction that their team captain, Dunga, signed with Reebok. I can remember early in the tournament when we realized that Dunga wasn't sporting the Integrity Pros, but instead a low-rent, barely leather version of a Reebok shoe that you could buy at your local Sears or JC Penney. It turned out that Reebok's Brazilian distributor had given him the bargain-basement boots instead of the top-of-the-line pair. Athletes being superstitious, once Dunga started wearing them and Brazil were winning games, there was no way that he was going to change to the superior shoe.

For the Brazil–Italy final, Fireman loaned me the Reebok company jet, so I could pick up Ryan Giggs in Boston and fly him to the Rose Bowl in Pasadena, for what still stands as the most stultifying nil-nil borefest in the history of the World Cup. After the Italian Roberto Baggio's penalty kick sailed into Row Z to end the shootout, Brazil and Dunga—still in the Reeboks you could buy for $29.99 almost anywhere in the Los Angeles area—lifted the trophy.

My epiphany during the final was one about the pace of change in America. Barely ten years earlier, 36 miles south in Long Beach, I had landed in what amounted to one of the nominal soccer "hotbeds" in America, with engineers and professors playing for fun and pride in front of hundreds at an abandoned American football stadium. And now here I was, one of the 94,174 there to watch the biggest sports event in the world. Soccer was finally, at long last, establishing its presence in the US.

◆

From early in the Patrick days, I had been traveling occasionally to Pakistan, where most of the world's soccer balls were constructed. We'd fly San Francisco to Paris, then Paris to Lahore, Pakistan, then take a sturdy 4x4 for the bumpy trip to a small town called Sialkot, in the disputed Kashmir region, close to the Pakistan–India border. As we made our way north, we would pass pick-up trucks, waving cheerfully and a little nervously at them as they were heading south from Afghanistan, laden with Mujahideen fighters, armed to the teeth with AK-47s and crates of ammunition, all paid for by the US government. The US saw the conflict in Afghanistan as part of the broader Cold War, and through Project Cyclone, funded the anti-Soviet rebels. Factions of the Mujahideen later joined the Taliban, and much of the weaponry supplied by the US was used against US forces in future conflicts in Afghanistan.

In this strange and mysterious world, we were always conscious of not trying to assert our own cultural biases. It's where the best hand-sewn soccer balls in the world were constructed. Milwaukee has beer, Silicon Valley has tech, Sialkot has soccer balls. As we were expanding the Reebok soccer line, I traveled back to Sialkot to sign a deal for soccer balls, part of our ambitious foray into broadening our range of gear.

All seemed to be going well as I attended the sporting goods Super Show in Atlanta in 1995, when I was informed that a reporter from CBS's Connie Chung show wanted to interview me for a piece about Reebok's growth in soccer. Had I been a bit more experienced or a bit more skeptical, I might have wondered why her investigative team at *Eye to Eye with Connie Chung* wanted to do a deep dive into soccer's growing presence in America, and Reebok's emergence.

I sailed into the interview blithely oblivious. I spoke about the craftsmanship of the soccer balls, and how the artisans in Pakistan who worked on Reebok balls were master craftsmen, exhibiting skills that had been passed down for generations.

Several weeks later, in early April, I was at home with my family as Tara, Tyler, and four-year-old Toni-Marie gathered around to see their dad on national TV. During the segment on *Eye to Eye with Connie Chung*, right after I made my comment about skills being passed down for generations, the piece cut away to a scene in Pakistan, and Chung's grave voiceover: "Peter Moore had no idea how far down the generations the mastery of craft has passed down..." What followed that voiceover was a powerful, damning exposé on child labor in the soccer-ball industry, and the entrenched nature of poverty in that region in Pakistan.

The reporting was solid. Though we regularly checked that those factories were observing the correct protocols, *Eye to Eye* reported the deeper truth, that many of those balls were constructed off-site, with child labor. It was not uncommon for factories to farm out their work, to drop off all the elements required for hand-stitched balls at someone's front door and then come back a day later to pick up the finished goods. Who was doing the off-site work, how much they were (or weren't) getting paid, and how long they were working were all unverifiable. We'd committed one of the cardinal sins of offshore purchasing—we had lost sight of the manufacturing chain.

I was mortified at my naivety of course, but also at our collective complacency. I'd been to those villages, heard the interpreters translate the platitudes from Urdu into English. But I hadn't looked closely enough at the larger reality. As it turned out, neither had anyone else in the industry. Subsequent reporting revealed that the same problem existed for Nike, Adidas, and all the rest. So this became not just a Reebok problem, but an industry-wide problem. Eighty percent of the soccer balls in the world were constructed in and around Sialkot, and *no one* was immune from the charges of child labor. The charges particularly stung at Reebok, where Paul Fireman had prided himself on the company's social conscience, and even had a department of human rights, headed by vice-president Doug Cahn.

"We're gonna sort this shit out," Fireman told me the next day, and at once I started working, with Cahn and with my own team, on how to solve the larger problem, My adroit executive assistant, Lori Larkin, had to figure out how to get me from Boston to Sialkot on an almost monthly basis. Once we got to Pakistan, it wasn't as simple as insisting that adults do all the work—in many families in Sialkot, the labor of the children was the difference between subsisting and not. We had to listen to the local leaders and begin to understand the scope of the problem. The solution involved not only self-contained factories, in which only documented adults could work, but also the infrastructure that would help get children out of forced labor—that meant schools, the beginning of athletic programs and a society that encouraged the development of children.

By this time I was chairman of the Soccer Industry Council of America, and we started the Task Force on Global Manufacturing Practices, and by the summer of 1996 the industry had mobilized to implement a new set of standards. In Sialkot, Reebok had established its own self-contained factory, which guaranteed that all production would come from workers 15 or older, that no children would enter the workplace, nor any soccer ball panels leave the facility during production, and that Reebok would support a program for education and vocational training for the children in the area.

Later that year, I traveled back down to Sialkot, along with our star women's soccer signing, the US women's national team star Julie Foudy, to observe the new factory. Within a year we'd made changes that earned awards for corporate responsibility. Instead of working in a sweatshop all day, the children of the workers at our factory in Sialkot were attending school. *Eye to Eye with Connie Chung* never came back to tell the rest of the story, but I felt satisfied that we had improved the lives of families in the region, lived up to Reebok's human rights charter, and made a bad situation significantly better.

◆

It is so much easier to admit and correct your mistakes in the professional sphere than it is in one's personal life. This is a hard truth I realized during the same period that we were putting out fires in Pakistan.

I had hit the ground running at Reebok, traveling extensively and working 60-hour weeks on the front lines of the sneaker wars. Bernice remained the ideal mother at home, taking care of our brood of three children. While the external trappings were all there—big house, nice salary, picturesque vacations—Bernice and I were increasingly distant, still locked into our respective roles. In February 1996, we were devastated when Tiffany, our fourth child, arrived stillborn. It was a time of immense shock and sadness. There was a somber funeral and we buried Tiffany's body in a cemetery in Medfield.

It was during this time that I committed the biggest indiscretion of my life, fathering a child outside of my marriage as the result of an affair with another woman. Alexandra was born in late 1996, something that I initially tried to hide from my family, before a letter from the probate court put paid to that futile attempt. I was ashamed, and devastated to have caused so much pain to my wife and created a crisis in our marriage. We agreed on counseling sessions and found a way, as difficult as it was, to maintain the family and manage through this rupture in our lives that I had created.

I didn't know if I could repair the relationship with Bernice. I was crystal clear on one thing: I wanted to stay with my family, couldn't imagine life without my children. So I compartmentalized my personal happiness, redoubled my efforts to succeed at work, and tried to make the best of it. I remember once reading an interview with the Who's Pete Townshend, describing his own childhood. He said his parents were never soulmates, weren't even suitably matched, but he appreciated that they stayed together for the sake of the children. That was what, in the end, Bernice and I vowed to do, and I hoped it was the right thing.

◆

In the years ahead, I would endeavor to completely lose myself in my work. And there was lots of work to lose one's self in. In the spring of 1996, Major League Soccer debuted, and I was on hand when San Jose's Eric Wynalda, sporting a pair of Reeboks, scored the first goal in MLS history. The launch of America's long-promised domestic soccer league was less auspicious. While there was a core of knowledgeable, soccer-loving people in key positions (including Lamar Hunt, who'd been an owner in the ill-fated North American Soccer League), it was clear that many of the decision-makers understood neither the game nor its burgeoning audience in the US. Which is why we got all the ludicrous team names—Dallas Burn, Kansas City Wiz, and the like—and gimmicky rules that only served to turn off the base of soccer-loving Americans. (Only with the arrival of Don Garber as commissioner in 1999, and the subsequent changes to a more authentic game, would the MLS begin to get a foothold in the States.)

In early July 1996, I flew to Liverpool for the press conference of my dreams, to announce that Reebok had signed a deal to be the official kit outfitter for Liverpool Football Club. Thirty-seven years and just a few hundred feet away from the place I'd stood as a four-year-old Scouser, I was announcing the Reebok/Liverpool deal in Liverpool's old trophy room, and introducing the new kit and leisurewear deal—which included the then-revolutionary change strip, in ecru (it was a French term, for "unfinished," and looked like a blend of cream and beige). Among the surreal events from that day was sharing tea with the Liverpool great, longtime left back Ronnie Moran—and making him feel quite old by informing him that he had been the captain on that day in 1959 when I first visited Anfield. I remember talking to the assistant coach Sammy Lee as well, and hearing how excited he was about the move to Reebok. Those within the club had felt (and rightly so) that Adidas had been phoning it in in recent years, putting Liverpool in the identical generic kits that other clubs and national teams were sporting. Reebok was a radical departure.

From there it was back to the States to gear up for the Summer Olympic Games in Atlanta. Reebok had been awarded one of the major corporate sponsorships, and we used that as a platform to assert our presence in the shoe market. (Nike, responding nimbly, bought billboards all around Atlanta, emphasizing the stars they had as well as their ethos. One billboard read, "You don't win silver. You only lose gold.")

But for that fortnight, the Reebok vector was everywhere. We established the Reebok Olympics Center in downtown Atlanta, a repurposed venue that we turned into a combination hospitality suite/media center/concept store. It was where Julie Foudy showed up with her gold medal the day after the US national team—one of the sensations of the Summer Games—won the women's soccer tournament, hinting at triumphs to come.

All of this was building up to France 1998, by which time we would be ready to assert ourselves, going toe to toe with the giants. A lot had changed in four years, since USA '94.

For one thing, the going rate for athletes wearing shoes had gone up to $1,500.

My dominant memory of France '98 was the surprise success of Paraguay, who'd qualified for the final 16 behind captain and goalkeeper Jose Luis Chilavert, who was also renowned for taking free kicks and penalty kicks for the side. I was commuting regularly between Boston Logan Airport and Paris Charles de Gaulle Airport during the tournament, and on the eve of the knockout round, I returned to France with a huge bag of new soccer boots for the Paraguayans. Going through customs, I was asked what I had to declare. In a classic rookie mistake, I told the truth, explaining to the French authorities that I was a representative from Reebok, carrying important shoes for the Paraguayan national team. The Paraguayans, you may remember, were slated to play France in the Round of 16. The authorities looked at my papers, and looked at the shoes, and decided something must be amiss.

"Monsieur, there seem to be some irregularities. You must wait while we sort eet all out."

And there I sat, fuming, for the next six hours. I finally reached John McCluskey by phone at the Reebok HQ in Paris and said, "I'm screwed. They're not going to let me out of the airport with the shoes." Thinking quickly, McCluskey rang up FIFA's director of communications, the Englishman (and fellow Liverpudlian) Keith Cooper. Such a position is not usually associated with omnipotent powers, but all FIFA executives essentially had diplomatic immunity in whatever country the World Cup was being staged. Cooper drove out to de Gaulle himself, scolded the authorities and got me released, or else I might still be there.

We had three times as many players wearing Reeboks in '98 as we'd had in '94, and it was a promising time for the soccer brand. But even then there were signs that the larger effort was falling short. Reebok's big gamble in the

’90s—Shaquille O’Neal—hadn’t turned out as well as hoped. Shaq was a great personality, but the same lesson that people learned with Kareem Abdul-Jabbar, Bill Walton, and Moses Malone was true for Shaq: Even if the giant in question was personable, people don’t buy shoes just because seven-footers wear them. “Big guys don’t sell shoes” was a lesson I’ve never forgotten. Other gambles had failed to pay off as well, and in 1998, the spring orders for the all-important fall season had been disappointing. Reebok had made a charge, but Nike’s counteroffensive was decisive.

That October, the head of HR came into my office and explained that the company was initiating a massive reorganization, and many of the vice-presidents—including me, by then the senior vice-president of global product marketing—were being let go. I packed up the belongings in my office that week and, on my final day, went upstairs to Paul Fireman’s office, asked his assistant if I could see him for a minute, and went in and thanked him for the time.

“What do you mean?” asked Fireman. “Where are you going?”

“Uh, I’m fired,” I explained. “You let me go this week.”

“What?! No we didn’t,” he said, appropriately incredulous. He proceeded to tell me that I was to disregard the firing and that I still had my job. Later that day, yet another HR member showed up in my office and, as I was unpacking my belongings to stay, apologetically negotiated a new contract, which stipulated that if I was let go again any time within the next twelve months, the company would owe me additional compensation beyond the standard severance.

That came in handy just two months later, when the head of Reebok’s North American division (whom I was somehow reporting to, as the reorganized Reebok corporate chain of command resembled nothing so much as a plate of spaghetti), invited me out to breakfast and told me I was, again, being let go.

It was a bleak time. For two weeks, I went into Reebok's "outplacement center" in downtown Boston, where the company tried to help find placement for all the people it was laying off. It resembled nothing so much as an extended scene from *The Walking Dead*.

And then out of nowhere, one night at home in Medfield, about a week before Christmas 1998, I received a phone call from a Seattle headhunter named Rick Edwards, who introduced himself and then opened with a very simple question.

"What do you know about video games?"

CHAPTER EIGHT

BATTLEFIELD PROMOTIONS

On the phone that day, I explained to Edwards that all I really knew about video games was that I had bought my son Tyler a Sega Saturn console system the previous Christmas for the princely sum of $499 and was pissed off because I'd recently found out the company was discontinuing the system—no more new games, no more support.

"Ah, well, funny you should mention Sega," Edwards said. As it transpired, he was calling on *behalf* of Sega, the Japanese company that had been one of the major challengers to the video-game giants Nintendo and Sony. The company was looking for a senior vice-president of marketing for their North American subsidiary.

I asked the obvious question: "Why me? I've been working selling athletic shoes for nearly two decades."

The answer, when one thought about it, made sense. Sega had a fiercely loyal, legendarily finicky audience, comprised largely of teenage boys. At Reebok, I'd spent hundreds of hours analyzing, surveying, and contemplating how to reach out to that very same demographic.

There were some differences—not every video-game addict had high-end sneakers, and not every kid with a high-end sneaker habit had video games, but the Venn diagram overlap was substantial. All over the country, there were kids by the millions wearing high-end sneakers *while* they were playing video games.

I went to northern California to meet with the head of Sega of America, a cantankerous but lovable wheeler-dealer named

Bernie Stolar, who worked his way up from his early days operating a coin-operated video-game business in California to become one of the key executives at Sony America launching the PlayStation. Stolar said I'd be perfect for the job, but told me he needed to take me to Japan first, so I could meet the Sega executives face to face. Very important, he said.

So it was off to Tokyo, for a meeting at the Imperial Palace hotel, where I sat in a booth with a phalanx of Japanese executives. There was the president of the company, Shoichiro Irimajiri, who'd made his mark with Honda and had the best understanding of the West; there was Hideki Sato ("Big Sato"), the hyper-serious executive who had the final say on financial matters; and among the others was the sharp, influential developer Yuji Naka, who had been the creator of the original *Sonic the Hedgehog* game that was the most successful franchise in the entire company. At one point, explaining my background through an interpreter, I told the executives I'd been born and grew up in Liverpool, England. At the mention of the city, a woman in the next booth turned around and looked my way. I recognized her instantly. It was Yoko Ono; our eyes met, she smiled, then went back to what she was doing. A brief moment that will be forever seared in my memory.

On that visit, I sensed that the Japanese executives weren't entirely comfortable with Bernie, but they gave me the stamp of approval. With all that had happened in Boston, the decision to move back to northern California was easy. We eventually settled in a beautiful home on Belvedere Island, giving me a picturesque daily commute to downtown San Francisco across the Golden Gate Bridge. Bernice was happy to be back in California, and my remarkably resilient kids adapted to being West Coasters again.

◆

The early months of Sega were a time of full immersion, like going to a foreign country and having to learn the language from scratch. I must admit to some initial pangs of impostor syndrome, but I dedicated myself to study both the creation and consumption of video games. The industry had grown remarkably in the two decades since my father had brought a Pong game into the Red Lion to stir up business. So I played video games (Tyler was a big help in this regard), I read about video games, I met with video-game creators, marketers, and sales people, both inside and outside the company. The learning curve was intense and nuanced. Who was Acclaim? Who was Namco? Who was Activision? And why was almost every one of the best-selling games coming out of Japan? Somewhere during this process I realized, *Nothing I previously thought I knew about video games really pertained.*

One had to understand not only the players, but the domestic Japanese rivalries—Sony and Nintendo and Sega—while also understanding the way the business was growing so rapidly that even the biggest company in the world, Microsoft, was determined to get in on the action. It was evident to me that the industry was on the cusp of a massive inflection point, and that the internet—as it was poised to be for so many traditional industries—was setting up a sink or swim scenario.

While Sega had made its fortune in the arcades, it was by then decisively moving into the home video-game market. An earlier console, the Sega Genesis, had shown great promise on its release—and Sega had nine in-house studios creating games exclusively for the company—but it was soon outstripped by other advances in console technology. Then a similar fate befell the Saturn, although a poorly executed launch exacerbated those issues. Now Sega was working on a new console that would bring gaming online. The promise of this intrigued me.

In those early months at the company, I experienced

an epiphany. I remember looking at a beta version of the legendary Japanese game developer Yu Suzuki's new game *Shenmue.* It was unlike anything I'd ever seen, or even contemplated seeing, before. To play the game, you assumed the persona of the protagonist Ryo Hazuki, who must avenge his father's death, and travel around Hong Kong and beyond looking for clues. There were elements of violence—martial arts and street-fighting—in the game, but what set it apart was its free-form spaciousness. The open world that Ryo explored seemed to go on forever. And rather than operating at the breakneck speed of most video games, it rendered a world in which events happened in real time. Want to catch a train to the next town to hunt for more clues? The next one doesn't come for another 13 minutes. No speeding it up. Want to pass the time? You could go into the virtual arcade on one of the streets in *Shenmue* and play a game in the arcade or go order a Coke at the café while you waited. But whatever you chose to do, the train wasn't coming for another 13 minutes. It was an investment of time and care with a purpose, leading to an accretion of details that provided Ryo with the necessary clues. And it was different from any video game I'd ever seen before. I didn't feel like I was playing it. I felt like I was *in it.* I eventually realized that it was, in a word, art.

In playing *Shenmue,* I began to understand the stakes, the creativity, the brinksmanship of Sega's audacious plan. It was preparing for the release of a new console—the Sega Dreamcast— in the fall and this was the company's best (and perhaps last) chance to regain market share in the all-important, ultra-competitive console wars. Nintendo was well established in the field, and had a new console, the GameCube, in development, Sony was due to release its PlayStation 2 in the spring of 2000, and even Microsoft was moving into the console field, with the Xbox rumored to be readying for release in 2001.

The Dreamcast was going to be the first console in history with online capability, and a broad variety of functions unlike anything that had gone before it. The console had the Windows CE operating system, so it was much easier to program games for than the Saturn, and also possessed a NAOMI motherboard, similar to what was found in the arcades, so that those games could easily be transferred for home consumption.

In April 1999, in front of a packed house of magazine writers and other media people and gamers in San Francisco, I made the public teaser/pitch for the new console: The Sega Dreamcast would roll out that September, and revolutionize video games. "We're taking gamers where gaming is going," was my message. Capitalizing on the industry-wide penchant for numerical shorthand, we announced that the Dreamcast would launch September 9th—9.9.99. By then, we had locked down all the advertising on MTV's Video Music Awards to be broadcast the night of the Dreamcast's release. From there, it was a sprint to the day of release.

With one jarring bump. In the midst of the intense buildup, in June of 1999, Bernie Stolar was relieved of his duties as president. The official announcement was vague, but it was clear that Bernie's blunt personality had been rubbing the Japanese up the wrong way. So three months before the launch that would make or break the company's future, the president was out, and the new president was ... me. I received a call late one afternoon from Big Sato, who said simply, "I want to let you know that Mr. Stolar is no longer in his position. We would like you to assume his role as president and COO."

It was a classic case of battlefield promotion. I had been in the video-game industry for six months and suddenly I was *running* Sega of America. Of course, if Sega hadn't been 90 days out from the Dreamcast launch, they likely would have conducted a more rigorous search and picked someone with more experience. But I had bonded well with the company's intermediaries—including Makoto Kaneshiro, the embedded executive in San Francisco (who undoubtedly was an informant for Japan), whose office was across the hall from mine—and received good reviews for how we delivered the big rollout announcement in April.

It was clear that this was the chance for Sega to transcend all the bad publicity around the demise of the Saturn. In addition to the launch of the Dreamcast, we also boasted an unprecedented lineup of games. Typically, a new console rollout would be accompanied by eight to ten new games on the day of release. Between our nine in-house studios and the licensed games through third-party developers, the Dreamcast launch would include some twenty new games, the majority of which were based on new intellectual property. Almost every studio of consequence in the business—save Electronic Arts, which was gearing up for the following spring's PS2 launch—delivered a game. In addition to Sega's perennial hit Sonic the Hedgehog (*Sonic Adventure*, the first 3D Sonic game), there was the epic martial combat game *Soul Calibur*, racing games like *Hydro Thunder*, and sports simulations like *NFL 2K* and *NBA 2K* (with icons like Randy Moss and Alan Iverson signing on for the massive "It's Thinking" ad campaign accompanying the rollout).

In the weeks leading up to launch, as we started fielding orders from all the relevant buyers, it became pretty clear that we were going to do a staggering amount of opening-day business. That started me wondering where our opening-day revenues would land in relation to other entertainment releases. I did some checking, and realized that the movie *Stars Wars: Phantom Menace* had enjoyed the biggest opening 24 hours in movie history, grossing over $24 million in ticket sales. Based on our estimates, we were going to go well past that mark. I started talking about the Dreamcast launch being the biggest opening day in American entertainment media history.

On the day of release, 9.9.99, I was in New York City for the VMAs. That morning, I walked into the Toys R Us in Times Square. The executives at the chain were still peeved because they'd received only 30,000 consoles for their initial shipment (they'd wanted twice as many, but we were striving to balance our initial production run of about 300,000 consoles between all our major retailers). The line to get into Toys R Us that morning snaked around the corner, and the sight of people buying as many as a half-dozen games along with their console confirmed all our hopes. The VMAs that night were energetic and revelatory, with Run-DMC teaming up with Steven Tyler and Joe Perry for "Walk This Way" in the opener, and Snoop Dogg, Dr. Dre, and Eminem joining in on "Nuthin' But a 'G' Thang" on the close. At almost every commercial break in between, Sega was peppering the audience with variations on the "It's Thinking" campaign.

By the next day, back in San Francisco, it was clear that we'd not only broken the single-day record, we'd destroyed it, showing $99.4 million in sell-through revenue. This was big news in the mainstream media, which was just then starting to grasp the broad reach of the video-game business. Sega's numbers remained encouraging all the way through the Christmas season and a bit beyond, as we were selling consoles as quickly as we could produce them.

And yet it turned out not to be enough. The PlayStation 2 dropped the following spring of 2000, easily breaking the one-day sales record we'd set just six months earlier. For all the success and positive publicity—more than a quarter-century later, the titles that rolled out with the Dreamcast's release still comprise the greatest launch lineup of games in video-game history—we didn't sell enough consoles, and when Sony flooded the market with the PlayStation 2, we were instantly marginalized.

Sony played it shrewdly in its rollout, pushing its own product but also waging a not-so-subtle, almost political, campaign of FUD—fear, uncertainty, and doubt—against us. I read so many interviews where Sony execs dismissed us as a "transitional" console. EA's refusal to devote any of its development resources to the Dreamcast certainly hurt as well.

By the summer of 2000, the existential challenge was clear—we needed to move the consoles to get more people on our SegaNet platform of online gaming. But during the 2000 holiday season, console sales were drying up. If you hadn't bought a Dreamcast before the launch of the PS2, you probably weren't *going* to buy one. Right after Christmas, I was summoned to Japan. The company was hemorrhaging money, with losses over a half-billion dollars for the fiscal year, the fourth straight year Sega had lost money.

The solution was obvious, and painful. On January 31, 2001, I led a global conference call with over 600 participants listening in, announcing that after less than eighteen months, the executives in Tokyo had decided to discontinue production of the Dreamcast and drop out of the hardware business altogether. Going forward, Sega would be a software-only company, operating as a pure third-party publisher. It was the single most difficult day of my professional career, having to tell more than fifty people there at Sega of America, with whom I'd worked side by side for two years, that they were immediately out of a job.

Added to the sad pall that hung over me in 2001 was the passing of my father Terry, who had suffered a debilitating stroke a year earlier and never recovered. It was difficult to see such a previously energetic and lively soul diminish into a mere shell of that person, but his memory lives on to this day in everything I do.

Back to Sega. We pivoted as quickly as we could. And I had the rather mortifying and humbling task of going to the very people we'd been competing with so feverishly in the previous year—Sony and Nintendo among them—and asking for dev kits so we could start producing games for those platforms.

Two things were true: The Dreamcast's launch was a critical success, and spawned some classic video games. But the other competitors had more money, more resources, and more games that tapped into the zeitgeist. We'd come up short, and in the high-stakes video-game business, that spelled severe consequences.

As we moved into the post-hardware future, we set a series of targets to achieve profitability, which inevitably included a large write-down of losses on the Dreamcast. With the Japanese brass, I negotiated a promise of bonuses for the entire company if we achieved those targets in the next fiscal year. It wasn't easy, and morale was understandably rock bottom. We had to mark down the Dreamcast—first to $149, eventually to $99—to clear out our warehouses and ramp up software sales. By the summer of 2002, we had achieved those targets and I congratulated the staff, only to be told by Big Sato (by then the president of the company) that we had somehow cooked the books and wouldn't get our bonuses. This was ludicrous on its face—there had always been an understanding that there would be a write-down on the losses with the console. I pushed back and threatened to quit on the spot if Sega didn't keep its word and pay the bonuses. Ultimately, the company agreed to do so. But it was a showdown that hinted at deeper troubles.

By that point, several things were coming into focus. The excitement over the Dreamcast's launch had obscured the larger story, the gradual loss of relevance and cachet that Sega had suffered over the previous decade. That summer of 2002, I started a series of focus groups and market studies to try to explain to the home office the severity of the problem.

The focus groups, run by Foote, Cone & Belding, had

brought a representative cross-section of gamers into a conference room in San Francisco and asked them about their habits and attitudes toward different companies. One of the key questions was, "If the company was a person, what kind of person would it be?"

I sat in on the sessions behind the one-way mirror. The answers were illuminating: EA was "the jock, six-foot-four, good-looking, dates the head cheerleader, kind of arrogant but popular anyway." The ascendant Take Two Interactive (whose subsidiary Rockstar was responsible for the wildly successful *Grand Theft Auto* series) was described by one gamer as "your crazy uncle, who shows up after a weekend in Vegas with a woman of ill repute; crazy but fun."

Then there was Sega. I still remember one of the more telling quotes: "Sega's your grandfather; he used to be cool, back in the day, but now he's just lame."

I brought the results to a meeting in Japan in the fall of 2002, armed with both the problem as well as a solution, a "gamer's manifesto" that I'd prepared with our team, which amounted to a way back to video-game relevance and profitability.

I started with the bad news, and I could immediately feel the tension rise in the room. As I was showing the videos from the focus group, I could see Yuji Naka—the brains behind the original *Sonic the Hedgehog* game—growing more and more incensed. It was an instructive experience in cognitive dissonance. The comments went down like a turd in a punchbowl. He couldn't bear the reality of the message this was delivering, so he blamed the messenger.

"This is wrong," Naka said through our translator.

"It's not wrong," I countered. "We've seen these trends for a long time."

"No one really thinks that way about Sega," Naka said.

"They do, and the focus groups are a representative sample," I said. "You saw the video."

"The video is doctored," Naka insisted. "You have meddled with the results."

At this point, the red mist came over me. The stress and frustration of the previous three years came to a raging boil. I looked at Naka, then turned to the translator and said, "You can just tell him to go fuck himself."

The translator looked abashed. "Moore-san," he said to me, "there is no word in Japanese that corresponds to that."

"I'm pretty sure there *is* a word in Japanese," I said. "Go ahead and tell him."

And I walked out. End of meeting. I was so frustrated by the pig-headedness that, on the long flight back to the States, I called our marketing chief, Mike Fischer, on the airplane phone. The first and last time I'd used such a ridiculously expensive device. I told him it was *his* turn to go and present the Japanese with the solutions that I never got to deliver.

Fischer was the ideal person to convey this message. Video gaming was in his DNA. He'd worked his way up through the industry by moving to Japan right out of college, learning Japanese, and understanding the culture. So he flew to Japan a week or so later and came armed with a PowerPoint full of hard truths that the Sega people needed to hear, but also the solution, as articulated by our "gamer's manifesto."

Our key points were:

- The gaming market had changed over the previous decade, and it wasn't just about teenagers anymore.
- Because adults had started playing in larger numbers, and the graphical power of the machines was improving in leaps and bounds, that meant there was an audience for more mature and complex games, like *Grand Theft Auto.*
- Sega's rich arcade heritage had started to hold the company back. Those games were not as effective in the home market, where people could finish a game over the course of a single weekend.

- In the American and European markets, there was more desire for multi-player games (like the wildly successful *Final Fantasy VII*), that took advantage of the larger living spaces in the West, and the growing online community.
- Finally, the brilliant game designers in Sega's nine in-house studios had become an isolated, jealous bunch of prima donnas, who didn't give us any information—or offer us the chance for any feedback—until their games were all but finished being built. In the modern world of video gaming, the best games started teasing, with meaningful assets, years in advance. But with the in-house studios, we often weren't privy to anything about the game until it was already in an alpha version, just a few months before release. It was maddening for the people trying to sell the games. We simply were not trusted to engage with the developers in the early stages of the creation of the games and provide input from the marketplace.

Fischer made all these points, carefully and constructively. But you won't be surprised that the executives were no more receptive to Fischer's news than they had been to mine.

"You just want us to make pornos!," Naka protested, spittle forming at the corners of his mouth as he got angrier. He was using as an example Tomonobu Itagaki's *Dead or Alive* games, which utilized titillating graphic depictions of statuesque female characters. "We are not going to make porn games, and who are you to tell me how to make games?!"

We had accurately described the problem, and we had given them a road map for how to fix it. But they were not to be swayed.

It was during this tumultuous period that I was asked to represent the video-game industry at the

McCain–Lieberman Senate hearings on Capitol Hill. A bipartisan group of senators had launched attacks on the entertainment industry, and Strauss Zelnick, then CEO of BMG Entertainment, representing the music industry, the legendary Jack Valenti, president of the Motion Picture Association of America, and I testified on behalf of our respective industries, which were under attack from small-minded and ill-informed senators who were blaming us for all sorts of societal ills. It was a milestone moment for the entertainment industry and ourselves in video games. We made our points clearly and firmly in the hearings and agreed to create more robust ratings systems for our respective media, but did not back down on the freedom of our creators to develop and distribute music, movies, and games that appealed to a mature, discerning audience.

Back in San Francisco, still furious at the intransigence at the Sega home office, I got a call from Robbie Bach, president of the Entertainment and Devices division at Microsoft. He said he wanted to talk, and asked if I could possibly fly up to Seattle for a meeting.

Everyone knew Microsoft was moving even more aggressively into the global gaming business, but they were still a bit of an enigma at this point. On my visit to Seattle, I had a meeting with Microsoft CEO Steve Ballmer, merely one of the richest and most powerful men in the world.

"We don't have anyone like you here," Ballmer told me. "We *need* someone like you. Someone who can throw punches."

The offer Microsoft made was for me to work as the corporate vice-president of home entertainment, focusing on the next iteration of the company's Xbox. In some ways, it was an echo of the move I'd made from Patrick to Reebok, as I would be going from the respected but cash-strapped outsider to a major player on a much larger scale.

It wasn't a tough decision to make; I'd spent nearly three

years as the stubborn *Gai-jin,* banging heads with the even more stubborn Sega execs.

I flew home to San Francisco, walked into the house and asked my family, “Do you like rain?”

CHAPTER NINE

THE LIVING ROOM WARS

To understand the environment I was walking into in 2003 at Microsoft, I think you have to understand how ludicrous it was to find the behemoth Microsoft—the most successful and least hip of all the tech companies—in the gaming space in the first place. I had nothing but respect for Microsoft's leaders, Bill Gates and Steve Ballmer. But they were, almost literally, the stereotypical nerdy guys with the pocket protectors—responsible for one of the unintentionally funniest YouTube videos of all time, dancing on stage to the Rolling Stones' "Start Me Up" to celebrate the launch of Windows 95.

Microsoft's venture into gaming came at the behest of Gates, who would turn out to be by far the smartest person I've ever had the privilege of spending quality time with. A polarizing figure in today's world, thanks to the ridiculousness of conspiracy theories powered by the Wild West of social media, I found Bill to be alien-like in his deep understanding of the critical issues in this world, especially global health, and his willingness to use his immense wealth to try to provide positive solutions. At the apex of Microsoft's domination—when the company was operating under a consent decree while the government was considering breaking up its supposed monopoly in the tech sector—Gates looked at the future and recognized that Sony, already dominant in televisions, DVD players, and audio equipment, was beginning to take over living rooms with the advent of the PlayStation console (and the potential for newer consoles to be smart hubs for all sorts of other audio-visual activities in the future). Gates realized that multimedia game consoles would be crucial to where technology was heading. He didn't want Microsoft to get left behind in the office.

"We can't let Sony control the living room," became the mantra.

The launch of the original Xbox, in 2001, had shown how naïve the company had been about the gaming industry. The console lacked power and storage (64 MB of memory and a 10 GB internal hard drive) and it was being marketed not all that differently than Microsoft marketed its other products. But to belabor the obvious: The strategy for selling a console to a hardcore gamer is quite different than selling Microsoft Excel and Outlook to the head of a big company's purchasing department. That's where me and the newly formed Xbox team came in.

The Microsoft campus in Redmond, Washington, just outside of Seattle—500 acres, with 50,000 employees at the time—was virtually its own city, with its own customs and rhythms. It was crawling with bright, stressed-out, socially awkward people speaking in an arcane jargon of acronyms. On my first day on the job, I went to an NEO (New Employee Orientation) with 190 other people who were starting work the *same day*, and was issued a guide with hundreds of other acronyms I'd need to learn to converse with the rest of the company.

Thankfully for me and the rest of the creative team, the entire Xbox home entertainment division was located about ten miles away at the Millennium campus, far away from "the Borg" in Redmond. Our mini-campus was a nondescript industrial park out at the end of the freeway, hard by a massive gravel pit. It was a charmless location, but we were happy to be there. We were the rebels, the creatives, the art-school kids left to our own devices. Millennium had a completely different ethos that was there for all to see—starting with the Jolly Roger pirate flag that flew near the entrance of the campus.

We would still go to the Borg periodically for meetings with Gates or Ballmer, but Xbox was intentionally set apart from the rest of the Microsoft empire. One of the efforts that started before I arrived and continued after I came on was a conscious decision internally that the Xbox team distinguish itself from Microsoft as a separate entertainment brand. To that end, Robbie Bach—who'd originally been senior vice-president of entertainment at Microsoft—became "Chief Xbox Officer," even though he was doing the exact same job. Everybody on the management teams was issued business cards with the Xbox logo, rather than the Microsoft logo, and email addresses with xbox.com extensions rather than microsoft.com extensions.

•

Among the first decisions made, by the end of 2003, was to discontinue the production of the original Xbox. It was already famously underpowered and outmoded, and the attach rate for games wasn't enough to justify continuing. In complete contrast to the basic tenets of business, the more consoles we sold, the more money we lost. When the final accounting was written, it would go down as a loss in excess of $5 billion, but it got Microsoft into the game console universe.

Plans were already afoot to build a better, more powerful, more online-friendly console, which would have to be the game-changer that Microsoft had been hoping for. We didn't have a title yet, but we had a codename for it—Xenon—and an idea that in addition to playing games in higher definition than ever before, it would also have to be highly powerful and highly versatile. We wanted Xenon, when it finally came to market, to be able display digital photos on your television screen, play CDs, rip CD tracks onto the hard drive as well as burn CDs onto blank discs, and play DVDs. Finally—if the consumer had broadband—the console would offer access to Xbox Live, which would eclipse SegaNet to become the world's best online gaming experience. We were doing away with a telephone connection, a huge gamble as we were building the hardware at a time when 80 percent of the world was still on dial-up. If you weren't broadband bound, bluntly you weren't our customer.

What followed was a two-year race for the most ambitious launch in gaming history. Our executive team—Robbie Bach, myself, and J. Allard (co-founder of Xbox, who was already a legend at Microsoft for his 1994 memo, "Windows: The Next Killer Application on the Internet," which Gates would cite as a key influence in the company's aggressive push into the internet realm)—was working feverishly with a team of about 500 super-smart geeks on the Millennium campus, and many third-party partners across the world, to roll out a revolutionary console with a formidable game lineup to go with it.

We had billions of dollars at our disposal, but that still required prioritizing where we'd put the capital. One week, Robbie brought the team together at the Willows Lodge in Woodinville, Washington, for two days of intense planning. He'd created a great visual tool for the exercise: A pile of about forty oversized "hundred-million dollar bills" as well as some small-change $50 millions, which we then had to apportion to various areas—hardware, peripherals, third parties, Xbox Live, marketing. The point here was clear. We could spend a lot of money on any number of areas, but even at Microsoft resources were finite and required discernment. Do we put more power in the console or spend more investing in third-party games? Do we invest more in peripherals from the very start or pour those millions into the advertising rollout?

Along the way, I was becoming the "face" of Xbox 360, the person trotted out at major media events and press interviews. At E3 in the spring of 2004, we announced the partnership with EA Sports—featuring an appearance by Muhammad Ali, who was greeted with a stirring standing ovation upon being introduced. With the entire industry clamoring for news on *Halo 2*'s release date, I walked onstage, rolled up my sleeve and showed a tattoo, reading "November 9" above the *Halo 2* logo.

Although, at this point, a true confession is in order: To borrow a song title from the Magnetic Fields, "I'm Crazy For You (But Not That Crazy)." The tattoo was actually an intricate bit of cosmetic work by the Hollywood makeup artist Eden Orfanos, who spent three-and-a-half hours making it look realistic, going so far as to have a slight reddening around the edges of the "tattoo," like someone who'd just been freshly inked. It needed to withstand scrutiny for the entirety of the show and for weeks beyond. And it did, speaking volumes about Eden's skill, and my ability to smile and nod when challenged as to whether it was real and whether I was actually daft enough to have a video-game release date tattooed onto my body. I know this may amount to a major disappointment to many gamers, as over the years I have never confirmed nor denied said ink on my body, but permanent branding was ultimately not an option. But real or fake, it certainly served the purpose of getting everyone's attention to *Halo 2* and *GTA IV*, and was symbolic of the irreverent fun and high jinks we had in the industry during that period.

By the beginning of 2005, we'd settled on a design—a sleek, vertical console, with a concave, customizable front (allowing gamers to put on their own personal faceplates) and tapered sides—and a name, the Xbox 360. That spring, we were prepared to prime the pump for the November launch. We got the actor Elijah Wood to host a half-hour special on MTV, a live spot at the Avalon Ballroom in Hollywood, with the Killers playing live. The draw for the special was the public debut of the console. In front of a packed, suitably enthusiastic crowd, a young woman walked onstage with a satchel, and took out the actual console—seen in public for the first time—to wild applause. Later that month Gates was on the cover of *Time* magazine, holding an early version of the console, and raising awareness and interest for the coming launch.

The work was nearly nonstop, but on Wednesday, May 25 of that year, I cleared my schedule for a long lunchbreak in the conference room at the Millennium campus. Liverpool's shaky but resilient side, without a true scoring threat in the front line, but powered by the rare brilliance of Scousers Steven Gerrard in midfield and center back Jamie Carragher, had advanced all the way to the final of the Champions League, in an unlikely bid to win their fifth European club championship. In Istanbul, they were facing the powerful, favored AC Milan. Soccer was probably more popular in Seattle than most places in America—the Sounders had been successful all the way back in the '70s in the NASL—but it was still a niche sport.

In total, about fifty colleagues joined me, knowing my love for Liverpool, but also lured by the beers and pork pies I'd ordered in bulk from the local British pub in Redmond. If you're reading this, you probably know the rest of the story: Liverpool were outclassed in the first half, giving up a goal in the first minute of play, and two more near the end of the half, to go into the intermission trailing by a seemingly hopeless 3–0 scoreline. I was bereft, and the nervous co-workers who'd joined me were unusually quiet, as our midday party had turned into a solemn wake. A couple people said they had to get back to their work and left. I stayed because that's what you do. Then Gerrard's header in the 54th minute made it 3–1, followed by two more goals in shockingly short order and suddenly, the "Miracle in Istanbul" was on. By the time goalkeeper Jerzy Dudek astonishingly parried two point-blank shots from Andriy Shevchenko in extra time, our collective shouts and yelps and expletives had drawn even more attention throughout the building. Dudek's masterful performance in the penalty-kick shootout lifted Liverpool to their most unlikely European Cup ever. It was a glorious celebration that lasted well into the afternoon. The next morning, hangovers subsiding, it was back to work on the Xbox 360 rollout.

"A Living Entertainment Experience Powered by Human Energy," was our mantra—I'm sure I repeated that in dozens, if not hundreds, of interviews. The rollout was a full-court press. We had directed a few of those "100 million dollar bills" to the advertising campaign, and one of the biggest parts of the budget was having McCann-Erickson develop a series of high-concept commercials to herald the launch of the new console. To emphasize the immersive experience of the Xbox 360, we developed the tagline "Jump In," inviting people to try out the first hi-def gaming experience.

One of the McCann-Erickson spots, titled "Standoff," was set in a busy train station. As the scene unfolded, a couple of guys look at another guy the wrong way, and soon they square off. One puts up his hand in a shooting motion, and the other two respond in kind. Soon the whole area is full of people aiming at each other—empty-handed—in the universal imitation of pointing "guns" that we all played as children. In the spot, as soon as one person "pulls the trigger," the entire place goes up in imaginary conflagration, while the Mills Brothers' "Tiger Rag" plays in the background. It was evocative, innovative, and wildly funny if you were at all familiar with the norms of gangster movies. And it never got shown on network TV. Before we could run the spot, we heard through channels that Wagner Edstrom, the London firm handling much of Microsoft's corporate communication, objected to the spot, arguing that it was "beneath" Microsoft to air a commercial so suggestive of gun violence. I was beyond furious, as I truly believed that the ad resonated brilliantly with our target demographic, but the ad was pulled. (I'd dealt with concerns about violence before, particularly during the testimonies in front of the Senate in 2000 while I was the head of Sega. What was frustrating was that video games were competing with every other form of entertainment—movies, graphic novels, television—and yet in many cases we alone were being held to a different standard.)

Other commercials did make the air, and for our launch date we rented a big airplane hangar out in the desert in Palmdale, California, and invited a few hundred gamers to join us for "Zero Hour," where they could stay overnight and play with the Xbox, and then be first in line when the consoles went on sale on November 15. The new console was indeed revolutionary, with ten times as much memory as the original Xbox, and 25 times the storage capacity. At BestBuy stores, they were showing off the new generation of hi-def TVs by bringing the Xbox 360s over and hooking them up to the TV sets. Within days, the console—selling for $399 at stores—was in such demand that it was selling for five times that amount on resale platforms.

We knew Sony would come out strong with the launch of the PlayStation 3 in the spring of 2006, but we'd accomplished what we'd wanted—establishing Xbox 360 as its most serious rival, and making clear that Microsoft was in the gaming space to stay.

I remember the entire leadership team reacting with incredulity when Sony announced it was charging $599 for the PlayStation 3, because we knew that price point would only steer more people to the Xbox 360. Their arrogance in their position in the market led them to state "gamers will work overtime in their jobs to afford a PlayStation 3." Turns out that wasn't the case, and I felt proud of what we as a team had accomplished, and our confidence grew with each week as the sales numbers came in. "First to ten million wins," was my belief and ultimately my external battle cry.

◆

E3 2006 saw the debut of another "tattoo," this time on my left arm, heralding the arrival of the *Grand Theft Auto* franchise to the Xbox 360. Things were going well in the battle against Sony. But by the fall of 2006, when *Halo 3* dropped, to continue another strong holiday season, we were starting to get some worrying feedback from customer service. All machines have failure rates, whether they're refrigerators, automobiles, or video-game consoles. But our failure percentages were becoming alarming. When it was operating correctly, the Xbox 360 console lit up with four connected arcs forming a green circle. But when the machine failed, the front of the Xbox showed those green arcs turning red. And a lot of gamers were experiencing that maddening failure signal, what they would soon start describing as "the red ring of death."

Todd Holmdahl, the smart, stoic hardware chief who oversaw all of the Xbox's insides, grew increasingly stressed as these reports came in. The problem wasn't merely that we had a problem. The problem was we couldn't figure out *what was causing the problem.*

At first it seemed a heat-related issue (some gamers were wrapping their Xbox 360 in a heavy bath towel, as a way to absorb the heat, or to redirect the heat back to the motherboard to melt and reseal cracked solder points). We were getting criticism from consumers and even more from retailers. Anyone whose console was still under the one-year warranty could bring it in for an exchange. But there were BestBuys or GameStops that would call us saying they had

400 broken consoles in their warehouses that they wanted credits for.

As Holmdahl and his team relentlessly worked to try to fix the problem, I still had to bob and weave. We couldn't admit we had a problem until we figured out what was causing it and how to fix it. In early 2006, I remained vague, in an interview with *Electronic Gaming Monthly*: "The huge majority of gamers are having a trouble-free experience with the Xbox 360," I said. "The very small number that have problems are being immediately taken care of by customer support." Classic evasive corporate double-talk.

But the problem accelerated as we got into the 2006 Christmas season, the first holiday in which Xbox 360 would go head-to-head against Sony's PlayStation 3. We had the *Halo 3* release—exclusive to our console—to further spur sales, but by that time all of the people who had bought the Xbox 360 when it first came out were no longer under warranty. And so if their console failed after that one-year mark, they were technically out of luck—and understandably furious.

As criticism mounted, Robbie brought the whole management team over to his house for a long meeting in the basement. I argued that this was our "Tylenol moment," the equivalent of the position Johnson & Johnson was in during the crisis in 1982 when some unbelievably evil person was putting cyanide into bottles of Tylenol. Rather than hedging, or denying, or pretending the problem didn't exist, Johnson & Johnson pulled every Tylenol bottle in the country off the shelves, and went back to market later with a series of tamper-proof packaging alterations, restoring consumers' faith in the product.

We needed to restore consumers' faith in *our* product. Some people—over half the ten million consumers who'd purchased the console—were having no problems. But those who were, like my son Tyler, kept getting the "red ring of death" (he went through three different consoles in that first year).

In the fickle, hyper-competitive world of video games, we felt we needed to make fixing the consoles as seamless an experience as possible for customers. The team agreed that we should extend the one-year warranty for all console purchases to three years. And we needed to streamline the return process to make it as quick and painless as possible, so that anyone who experienced "red rings" could call us and we'd FedEx a container to return their console, then FedEx out a replacement as soon as we received the defective one. The cost would be astronomical, and it was left up to me to go to the Borg and pitch the idea to Steve Ballmer.

It was one of those meetings where I made no small talk, delivered no introductory joshing. Rather, I laid it out for Steve. I explained the urgency of fixing it not only to save the Xbox 360 but also keep the growth of Xbox Live on an upward trajectory. Quite frankly, it was about saving the Xbox brand from the ignominious fate of being tossed onto the scrapheap.

"What's it going to cost?," asked Steve.

I took a deep breath, looked him straight in the eye, and said, "About 1.15 billion dollars."

To Steve's eternal credit, he responded at once.

"Do it," he said

He recognized, as had the management team, that it was too important *not* to do it. On July 7, 2007, I published an open letter to gamers, apologizing for the manufacturing defects and extending the warranties of all Xbox 360s from one year to three years, and launching the return program. I was relieved that he agreed to the immense cost, delighted that we were salvaging our brand from the potential ashes of negative customer sentiment, and in awe of his decisiveness to resolve the issue, without the screaming and desk-pounding that I had feared walking into that meeting.

By then, Holmdahl and his team had already started making minor adjustments, many of them centering on the source of many of our troubles, a lead-free solder that was, after repeatedly melting in the heat and subsequent drying, rendering the consoles inoperable.

The bill wound up being $1.3 billion in the end, but it would prove to be a wise investment, rallying support and loyalty on the part of users, keeping Xbox 360 as a major player, and protecting the growing profile of Xbox Live's online experience. By the end of the following year, the customer satisfaction numbers among Xbox users were historically high. We'd saved the enterprise.

Though by the time the open letter was published, I was already off on a new adventure, which started in the spring with an email whose subject heading read, "Time to Come Home."

CHAPTER TEN

IT'S IN THE GAME

The recruiter who'd sent the cryptic email was representing Electronic Arts, one of the biggest and most important entities in video games. EA had grown rapidly—from a nerdy PC game called *Earl Weaver Baseball* in the late '80s—into an industry monolith, best known for its hyper-realistic licensed authentic sports games. EA was the industry's 800-pound gorilla, whose cooperation or lack thereof could make or break an entire console launch. Our inability at Sega to convince EA to develop a game for the Dreamcast in 1999 had been a significant setback; conversely, EA's decision to get on board with Xbox 360 in time for the 2005 launch had been a crucial factor in helping the console succeed. The Xbox's rollout was bolstered by the EA catalog of its wildly popular *FIFA* soccer game and *Madden* NFL game, and its breakthrough hit *Tiger Woods Golf*, which was using Woods's transcendent popularity to introduce a new generation and entirely new demographic to the sport. Along the way, the company's advertising credo—"It's in the Game" became nearly as pervasive as Nike's "Just Do It."

I was invited down to northern California to visit the company's CEO, the hard-driving, supremely smart John Riccitiello, with whom I'd been alternately fighting and partnering for much of the previous decade. Over drinks in the garden of his Woodside estate, Riccitiello sketched out a vision of the future in which he wanted me to play a key role.

John was a new breed of video-game executive, one who'd cut his teeth with more conventional brands—like Pepsi, Clorox, and Wilson—before coming to the video-game business as it was growing in scope, adding a sophisticated, hard-nosed business mindset to the equation. In 2004, he'd left EA to join U2's Bono in the venture-capital realm of Elevation Partners for a few years, but had just returned in 2007, after the board offered him the CEO job. EA was in an odd position—well known, with healthy revenue, but slow to come to grips with the rapidly changing mobile and online markets, and coming off its first non-profitable year. There were mounting problems: The company was badly overstaffed, and yet the game quality—for all the licenses and claims of authenticity—was often spotty, leading to a frequently irate customer base. Even the previously infallible *FIFA* game was being challenged by Konami's *Pro Evolution Soccer*, which despite its lack of all the best licensing deals was in many gamers' minds the more playable game, earning better scores in the all-important Metacritic ratings.

EA was far more than its sports brands; there was *The Sims*, the first big video game to really break through to a critical mass of female gamers, and also more conventional games like *Mass Effect* and *Need for Speed*. Riccitiello was switching the company to a more vertical "label" system, similar to music and movie conglomerates which divided their massive organizations into distinct silos. John wanted me to be the president of EA Sports, taking over the making, marketing, and rights negotiations for the company's established sports lines, which also included licensing agreements with the NBA, NHL, NCAA football, and NASCAR. He was very persuasive, offering me a challenge and a chance to combine my experience in the industry with my love of sports, and also return to northern California. It took me a couple weeks to agree, after more of the Riccitiello charm offensive and talks with Bernice, but I finally decided it was an opportunity I had to take.

Robbie Bach was disappointed I was leaving—we'd just emerged from the worst of the "red ring of death" fiasco and were building up the trust of our customer base once again, implementing the extended warranty and express delivery-and-return program. But he understood the opportunity that I had and wished me the best; meanwhile, I agreed to stay on through July and the E3 Show in Santa Monica to ease the transition at Xbox.

About two weeks before my final day at Xbox, Robbie graciously allowed me to attend a meeting with my new employer. I took a day off to travel to New York for what Riccitiello said would be an important crossroads in the history of the company. He brought in about 150 senior-level executives in the company, and we met in a conference room at the posh W Hotel in midtown Manhattan, where Riccitiello made a presentation designed to get everyone's attention.

It started with a distant shot of the ocean, then zoomed in close enough to focus in on an offshore oil-drilling platform.

Then the picture zoomed in a little closer and you could see the same platform going up in flames.

The metaphor wasn't difficult to understand. Riccitiello pointed out that some previously successful companies, even after seeing and smelling smoke on their platform, stubbornly refuse to change. Others risk it all, and jump into the shark-infested waters, slick with oil and burning flames, in an effort to find safe harbor elsewhere.

The physical production of games on discs and reliance on retailers to manage the relationship with the gamer, Riccitiello noted, was the burning platform. And EA was going to have to find a way to make the difficult transition to an online model that would meet consumers where they lived and played. After his presentation, John asked me to say a few words. I noted sheepishly that I was a tad concerned that I'd just been helicoptered *on* to the burning platform.

But I knew my mission. From SegaNet to Xbox Live, I'd spent much of the past decade trying to help persuade consumers that the future of gaming was going to be online. That would be the charge here, to convince loyal customers who were used to doing things one way to broaden their horizons and start doing them another way. And if there's one thing I knew about gamers at this point in my career, it was that they hated change.

So the family moved again. By then Tara and Tyler were well on their own, Tara doing absolutely brilliantly in her career in PR, and Tyler just graduating from college. Both were graduates of the University of California at Berkeley, where Tara had also rowed on the crew team. We were fortunate to be able to get Toni-Marie enrolled at Sacred Heart School in Atherton. We found a beautiful home on a tree-lined street, just north of Stanford and Palo Alto, and about 15 minutes away from work.

There aren't many places in the world better to work than the EA campus in Redwood Shores. It was as California cool as you could imagine, a halfway house between a lavish college dorm and the real world of work, with a massive atrium and a building that had a terrific gym and its own Starbucks, even a sports bar where we could convene after a particularly productive afternoon.

For the next few years, my life was mostly lived in the hub of the EA Sports campus, with frequent trips to Vancouver, where the studio that produced the *FIFA* and *NHL* games was located, and the studio in Orlando, where *Madden* and *Tiger Woods Golf* were being designed and constructed. Scattered in between these studio visits were trips to the NFL, MLB, NBA, and NHL league offices in New York City and FIFA headquarters in Zurich. All of this was ably pulled together by my indispensable right hand, Tana Billingsley, my executive assistant and a fellow Brit. Tana shared my acerbic sense of humor but also possessed brilliant administrative skills that helped me navigate the often rocky existence of being an executive at a major video-game publisher that charted new paths to monetizing gaming in the burgeoning digital environment.

Sports fans had been trying to simulate the strategy and tactics of their heroes for decades, often with complicated card games involving dice, data-dense player cards, and broad situational charts. But the genius of EA was its ability to simulate those games in real time, with a game controller allowing fluid play instead of the time-consuming dice rolls and cross-checking of the board games. For frustrated fans, the EA Sports titles allowed them to serve as head coach, star quarterback, striker, or Tiger Woods himself, sporting a red shirt, making a charge on a Sunday afternoon at St. Andrews or Pebble Beach.

In America, where the *NFL* and the *Madden* game were king, we carefully maintained our separate relationships with the NFL on one hand and the NFL Players' Association on the other. We'd visit the coaching and broadcasting legend John Madden each summer, sharing the developments and refinements we'd made on his game, many of which were suggested by Madden in earlier sessions. Then we'd bring the beta version to New York City to show the league. Commissioner Roger Goodell, to his credit, was keenly aware that *Madden* was a perfect introduction to pro football for a younger audience, and always attended the meetings, incredibly interested in the game's evolution. Same with David Stern at the NBA and Gary Bettman at the NHL. The commissioners knew all too well the critical role we played in engaging the next generation of fans, something they worried about intensely—and rightly so.

My first two years constituted a learning curve at EA. We tried very hard to get our loyal customers to branch out—to get *Madden* players to try out the *NHL* game, or *FIFA* players to take a chance on *Tiger Woods Golf* (and vice versa). But the truth was that they were loyal to the games they loved. Someone who lived to see how he would do as Peyton

Manning leading the Colts' offense just didn't have the same impulse to lead the Penguins' line as Sidney Crosby.

What we realized quickly was that branching out horizontally made less sense than trying to offer customers something more in the vertical space. It was around this time that some visionary team members in Vancouver came up with the idea of the Ultimate Team concept for *FIFA*. It offered players a chance to purchase superstars to assemble a veritable Dream Team. Rather than sticking with the static teams in the game that matched the real-life rosters, Ultimate Team offered nearly unlimited flights of imaginative team building. So if you always wanted to see whether Messi, Ronaldo, and Wayne Rooney would work well together, Ultimate Team offered you the chance to find out. The cost to build out the platform was estimated at $3 million, and initially I had no idea where we were going to find that in the budget, but we found it somewhere, and what a solid investment it proved to be. Within three years, it was generating an additional $100 million per year. To this day, EA does not break out in any detail the revenue for Ultimate Team, but the best analysts in the business put it at somewhere north of $1.8 billion. That was a supremely well-spent upfront $3 million investment that, equally importantly, enabled a deeper, richer engagement for gamers who yearned for more than just playing out the game with license-locked Premier League or Bundesliga teams.

This was the revolution in sports games, and the mammoth universe of *FIFA* was at the cutting edge. We already had 350 licenses—from leagues to federations to referees' associations—in the game, and at one point we had 15,000 players, each with six different attributes, and for some of whom we'd captured three-dimensional imaging, so they moved on the screen quite similarly to how they moved in real life.

Things were running along smoothly at EA Sports until late November 2009. One day around Thanksgiving we received an email from Mark Steinberg, Tiger Woods's agent, which said, cryptically: "You're going to read a bunch of things about Tiger in the news tomorrow. None of it is true." We were perplexed, though I have to say I'd been in the business long enough by this time to know that when an agent defended a client by saying "None of it is true," it frequently meant that *all* of it was true.

The next day, the story began to break about Tiger's myriad cases of infidelity, and his crashing into a fire hydrant after his wife Elin Nordegren used a nine-iron to smash a window in his vehicle. Within days, as the tabloids were filled with numerous accounts from various women who'd had affairs with Woods, he found many of his corporate partners abandoning him. Nike was silent, but didn't drop him.

At EA, we were in an impossible position. We were in the very finishing stages of *Tiger Woods Golf 2010*, to be released in the spring. Tiger was in virtually every frame. We retrofitted our moral position based on the practical considerations. I went on CNBC and made the point that, whatever Tiger's personal drama might be, he'd still transcended the sport and opened it up to an entirely newer and broader audience and we were going to stand by him. After laying out my position, I heard in my earpiece another interviewer—the CNBC business journalist Mark Haines from New York—who asked, "Peter, Peter ... if Tiger had *murdered* someone, would you still stand by him then?" I sputtered out some kind of a response to that. We went ahead and shipped *Tiger Woods 2010* but soon thereafter recognized we needed to take his name off it. The next year we renamed the game *PGA Golf*. It was the right move; it was the understandable move. Yet it was also true that the game never sold as well after that.

◆

On May 25, 2011, I was attending a board meeting at Timberland in New Hampshire, where I was an independent director, when I got a call from my son, Tyler.

"Dad," he said, "um, you were just on *South Park.*"

The words did not initially compute.

"*On*?" I said. "What do you mean I was on *South Park*? Do you mean EA was mentioned on *South Park*?"

"No, *you,*" he stressed. Shortly thereafter my phone and email started lighting up, as people from all over the country chimed in, having watched the "Crack Baby Athletic Association" episode, which featured the *South Park* kids making a trip to EA headquarters, where they encountered a caricature of me called Mr. Peters (with a Southern, rather than a British accent), who at the end of a brief conversation, told them, "Well, boys, this has been real educational and all, but now let's part with that old EA Sports saying, 'Get the fuck out of my building!'"

That mention was a completely random one-off, and hilariously funny in typically irreverent *South Park* style, but EA was facing a growing resentment in the air. The transition from physical discs to online delivery systems was trying for everyone in the industry, and as a leader, EA was becoming an easy target for critics. The problems were mounting, exacerbated by the negative publicity around the ending of the *Mass Effect 3* game. That same year, a website called The Consumerist had held a readers' poll and declared EA "the worst company in America." By then, John had taken over the chief operating officer role, in addition to his CEO role, and he seemed beleaguered.

Later that year, he called me into his office and offered me a promotion to be EA's chief operating officer. In the move to an online model, we'd not done a good job updating our billing systems—rather than dealing with several huge companies like BestBuy and GameStop, we were now dealing with millions of individual consumers, making relatively minuscule microtransactions, and we needed to find a way to make that process easier for them and less expensive for us. Meanwhile, the offshore call center that we had handling customer service was generating additional complaints about the customer service itself.

We were in the process of changing direction on a massive scale, and that is never done without stress or conflict. One reason John had tabbed me for the COO role was precisely because I was able to embrace difficult change while maintaining a certain *esprit de corps*. Sports isn't business, at least not in its purest form, and it can be misleading to equate the two. But there are some commonalities. A team is only as good as its weakest link, and the same is true for businesses. And the key to team chemistry is a feeling among leaders that everyone is being heard and recognized.

So I started a series of weekly meetings, dubbed "The Engine Room," to try to get everyone pulling in the same direction. I invited about fifteen senior executives, drawn from every division—publishing, marketing, finance, HR, operations, legal, and IT. They'd come in early every Monday morning, stopping by the Starbucks in the atrium, and we started to address the main issues the company was facing.

Some things were straightforward, like streamlining the billing systems. Others took more time. I moved our call center from an outsourced spot to one in-house, staffed in Austin, and another one in Ballybrit, a suburb of Galway in Ireland. That helped begin to turn around the perception of the company. I loved visiting both campuses, staffed by the most hard-working, patient, customer-focused individuals you will ever meet. Almost all hardcore gamers themselves, they could walk gamers with issues through the most complex of problems.

Meanwhile, I made my efforts to address the elephant in the room, the company's reputation. "The tallest trees catch the most wind," I said to more than one interviewer, by way of defense and explanation, before going on to point out that whatever the gripes were, EA remained an award-winning company whose games were often dominant in their respective spheres.

Around this time, I recognized that one of the problems facing EA was its collective corporate arrogance. You couldn't treat PR at a video-game company like you were Dow Chemical or IBM. I had been aware of the growing influence and reach of the social media platform Twitter. I finally convinced my head of communications, and great friend, David Tinson, to allow me to dive into the then relatively uncharted waters of social media. I created an account in October of 2012, with the entirely pedestrian initial tweet of, "If only my real Liverpool were as good as my FIFA 13 Liverpool."

I soon recognized that there was value to Twitter far beyond fretting about my beloved Reds. For hardcore gamers who paid attention to the industry, Twitter was a social space that put a human face on the large company. Engaging with gamers was a way to connect. There were far fewer trolls than you might expect at that time, and they appreciated feeling like their concerns were being heard, as well as getting updated on developments, release dates, patches, and such.

It was during this time that an old friend in the digital sports space, Brian Grey, reached out with an intriguing opportunity, and one that squarely played into my interest in the digital tsunami of sports fan engagement on the web. He was CEO of a growing San Francisco-based start-up called Bleacher Report, which was utilizing a crowdsourced type of sports journalism to bring stories which emanated from the fans as well as content coming from non-traditional sports journalism sources. I joined as the only independent director, and received an eye-opening crash course in what was to be the future of 24/7 sports content creation.

We spent the following year honing the platform, improving the quality of the content, and were eventually acquired by Turner Broadcasting for $175 million in the summer of 2012. More importantly, I could see the future of non-traditional sports journalism, and the power of the fan in the storytelling and narratives surrounding their favorite teams and players.

I was starting to get traction on the COO role at EA in the summer of 2013 when things came to a head between the board and John Riccitiello. He'd gone all in on preparing for the next generation of consoles, and those investments couldn't pay off until the consoles dropped. Both Sony and Xbox wound up delaying release and that soon spelled trouble for EA's bottom line. John left, as cordially as one could under the circumstances.

There was an extensive search for John's successor and I was one of three internal candidates, including my longtime colleague Frank Gibeau and the young Australian Andrew Wilson, who had been a rising star in the company for several years. On September 7, 2013, the company announced they were giving the reins to the young gun Wilson.

I was surprised and disappointed, but I could hardly quarrel with the choice (then or now, where Andrew remains the CEO and EA is performing well). It began a tough phase of my career, however. In 2015, Andrew moved me to the new title of chief competition officer, officially a lateral move that put me in charge of the company's e-sports efforts. He was certainly entitled to pick his team, but I sensed my role was diminishing at EA. The new position was less fulfilling than the earlier ones. While this was a growing part of the industry, I felt marginalized and relegated to a narrow silo of the business when I had been used to having an incredibly broad reach and sphere of influence as COO.

◆

As I was struggling to chart my future with EA, I was also encountering the consequences of my past.

I had tried, in my imperfect, furtive way, to stay in touch with my daughter Alex. During the 2000s, I started serving on the board of Timberland, which required occasional trips back East for meetings in Stratham, New Hampshire. On these trips, I'd occasionally coordinate with her mother to schedule meetings with Alex. I had been supporting Alex financially throughout her life, but now I found myself wanting to spend more time interacting, providing guidance when I could, to help her get through this tough period in her life.

One day in 2012, I was alarmed to find out that her mother had sent Alex off to a "rehab" school in Utah, to "straighten her out." Alex didn't want to be there and called me to see if I could help get her out, but of course my hands were tied. Through those years, though, we kept in touch and saw each other occasionally. As she struggled through those challenging years, I became more involved in trying to help her navigate bouts of immense self-doubt and outright depression. Eventually Bernice found out. I had broken the pact of non-contact, and this unsurprisingly created turmoil and anger.

Increasingly I couldn't see a way back. One of the reasons we'd stayed together in the past—to get the kids launched—no longer existed, as Toni-Marie had by this time left for college. I felt constricted and stuck, an essentially happy person in a profoundly unhappy place, both personally and professionally.

Something had to change. Soon enough, something did.

CHAPTER ELEVEN

MOMENT OF TRUTH

Inertia is a powerful force. After more than three decades of marriage, Bernice and I were stuck, but we kept trying to work through it. We sincerely—even heroically—tried to save our marriage. We began doing regular marital counseling sessions at lunchtime. I would rush out of work and drive up to Menlo Park, spend 50 difficult minutes discussing our relationship, then drive back to work feeling discouraged, not only about the state of my marriage, but about pretty much everything else as well.

I was not arguing with the basic facts that led us to counseling, nor the belief that I bore the lion's share of responsibility for the marital discord. But once that had been decided, and amends had been made, it still left the question: Now what?

Bernice had been a wonderful mother, but with no children around she was struggling to find her own sense of purpose. I turned 60 in 2015, and was cognizant of how precious time was. For my part, I wanted to do right by all parties involved, and not hurt anyone. But what I also wanted—and this was the first-generation American in me—was to find happiness.

Things were stressful at work, as EA continued to make the migration from physical to digital. Compounding this, I lost my beloved mother Marilyn that year. She had struggled with her health for a couple of years, and I felt blessed that I was able to get back to Wrexham to be able to hold her hand and whisper my love and thanks into her ear in her final hours. She still leaves a hole in our hearts that will never be filled.

In the midst of the pressures and anxieties at home and on the job, I lost myself in running. I'd get up early, and arrive at the EA campus at 5:30 in the morning, in time to take a long run north by the Steinberger Slough, in the San Francisco Bay. Out in the dim morning silence, with little more than the sound of the tide hitting the shore, I would run for five or six miles, recording it all faithfully on my Runkeeper app. I've always been a runner, since early cross-country races back in the '60s at Grove Park, and in this period I badly needed the psychological release. Somewhere along the way, the stress and worries and guilt and concern would slip away. I would recover my bearings and my zest for life and my sense of gratitude.

There were many blessings to count. Bernice and I had three healthy children in the process of successfully launching as adults. I had another child, born in difficult circumstances, for whom I felt a strong sense of responsibility. I lived in a beautiful home, had a solid career, and I was rich in friends. Even my life as a sports fan was rewarding. In the fall of 2015, Liverpool (still in a funk over their late fade in the 2013/14 season) had hired the charismatic German manager Jürgen Klopp, and while the early results were inconsistent, you could tell instantly that he was going to have a galvanizing effect on the club, instilling a new spirit into both the team and their supporters, as he turned us all, in his own words, "from doubters to believers." Meanwhile the Patriots and Red Sox—the teams I'd adopted during my time at Reebok—were both in a positive stretch.

So much else in life was unsettled. Driving back from another marital counseling session one day, I finally recognized the inevitable. Both Bernice and I had given it our all. But we had grown apart over the years, and the thing we had been striving to save didn't really exist any longer, and we both knew it. In the end, I wasn't angry, only resigned. For the first and only time in my life I was experiencing mental health issues, admittedly of my own creation, and I was in a bad place at what I knew was a crucial crossroads in my life.

I would seek the best and least painful way to extricate myself, but I realized then that we were inevitably heading toward a divorce. Both Bernice and I had worked too hard and too long to consign the rest of our lives to a joyless stalemate. I wanted, at least, to give myself a chance to find genuine happiness.

◆

Back in 2007, shortly after I started work at EA, the company hired a talented trade marketing director, Debbie Mills DuBois. She was one of a kind—a brainy Californian who exuded joy and positivity, possessed a raucous laugh, and easily adapted to whatever environment she found herself in. She didn't report to me, but I'd met with her and her team at one point, and came away impressed with her smarts and her resilience, as a successful woman thriving on her own terms in a largely male environment. During her time at EA, she led an innovative marketing approach to selling the *Madden* game, opening a self-contained EA satellite store in the middle of BestBuy's flagship store in Minneapolis. After Debbie left the company for other opportunities, we sporadically stayed in touch and I served as a reference for a couple of her jobs.

Late in 2015, she'd moved back to northern California, to be the director of trade marketing for GoPro. We'd been meaning to catch up and finally met up one day after work in the following spring at the Third Avenue Sports Bar & Grill—a nicely appointed sports bar right off the El Camino Real in San Mateo. Debbie was radiant, still the fiercely self-reliant woman I remembered: whip-smart, warm, and a force of nature in whatever room she entered. We discovered that day that our lives had been on roughly parallel tracks. In the intervening years since she left EA, she'd moved with her family down to Santa Barbara for a job with Sonos. But by 2015, she'd filed for divorce, and moved with her sons Brody and Remy—and her Great Dane, the beloved Diego—back up to northern California, to take the job with GoPro. Despite all the upheaval, she remained optimistic about the future. Debbie was a kindred spirit, wired for positivity, striving to live her best life, fearless in the face of any challenge. She breathed new life and energy into my soul. Not long after that we were firmly an item, and I was energized, optimistic, and upbeat once again.

In the late summer of 2016, I received a call from a recruiter. If you're an executive of any consequence, you get calls from recruiters every now and then. You always listen, but most of them come to nothing. This sounded like one of those. It was a call from Spencer Stuart, a highly respected executive search firm, and this call was from their London office.

"Would you ever consider moving back to England?," the woman representative asked.

This was an easy no. I was just ending a 33-year-long marriage and was in love with the quintessential California girl, who'd been living in the Golden State since the age of 10.

"No way," I replied.

"Okay, but," said the recruiter, "what if it was to be ... the CEO of Liverpool Football Club?"

Well now. What flashed in my brain was the saying, *Never say never.* I told the recruiter that I'd need more information, but that was one job that I'd at least be willing to discuss.

Though I'd been a fan for life, I'd never officially worked for the club. But I knew so many people who were or who'd been at LFC, starting with my old youth teammate Joey Jones. I'd also been close to the club as far back as the mid-'90s kit deal with Reebok. In 2010, I'd first met the Liverpool (and

Red Sox) owner John Henry, shortly after he led a consortium to purchase the club. We'd had a meal and a meeting at the Mandarin Oriental Hotel in Boston, where he and his wife Linda were living temporarily while their Brookline home was under construction. It was a few weeks after he bought the team and was studying up, watching a '70s era video showing King Kenny Dalglish in his pomp, and trying to fully comprehend what he'd gotten himself into.

There had even been some feelers back then about whether I might be interested in the CEO's job. I passed at the time, because president of EA Sports was a great job, and I felt a deep loyalty to John Riccitiello and what we were accomplishing there. But now, several years later, many things had changed. I had a different role at a different EA, and John was long gone.

I eventually met, at a rather clandestine meeting in their London office, with a senior partner at Spencer Stuart and he explained that the set of parameters for the job kept moving. But I was interested, and what began shortly thereafter were a series of furtive conversations between myself and Mike Gordon, the perceptive, soft-spoken president of Fenway Sports Group, the Boston-based consortium which owned Liverpool FC, the Boston Red Sox, and other sporting endeavors.

As the Spencer Stuart recruiter had warned, Liverpool was in the midst of changing the definition of the CEO's role, moving to what Gordon described as "svelte CEO" or "skinny CEO." There was a better sense of what the job *wasn't* than of what it was. I had been used to Silicon Valley's exhaustive taxonomy, in which every executive job included multiple pages of roles and responsibilities. FSG's vision for the new CEO was a couple paragraphs of word salad that was best distilled at the time as, "everything but the buying and selling of players."

The new corporate hierarchy had Gordon, based in

Boston, as the de facto chief, with four different executives reporting to him directly: Jürgen Klopp was in charge of the first team; Michael Edwards was the sporting director, responsible for player acquisition and off-loading, as well as the sporting operations; the bright American Billy Hogan was chief commercial officer, handling the club's corporate partnerships. Meanwhile, the new Liverpool CEO would be solely responsible for all off-the-field business, ranging from gameday operations to corporate communications to supporting sponsorship deals to fan engagement and the like. In the broadest of terms, the CEO would be responsible for day-to-day operations, and for maximizing revenue that could then be turned over to the football side of the club to acquire new players and pay the ones already at the club, but he would have no say in those decisions.

In early October, I flew out after work to Chicago for another interview with Mike Gordon. We had already had numerous conversations about both personal and professional values, and how my experience in the video-game industry might help LFC face some of its challenges. Meeting in a suite at one of the O'Hare Airport hotels, Gordon talked to me for two hours, and never formally offered me the job, though he behaved as though I'd already accepted. At the end of the night, when we'd sorted through all the relevant details, Gordon declared, "All right, good. We'll get going on everything." We shook hands and I headed back to the terminal.

While waiting for my flight, I called Debbie and said, "Well, I *think* I've got the job. I mean, I know I've got the job, but there was no definitive declaration." That would come in due course, and by then all the theoretical discussions that Debbie and I had engaged in were couched in reality. Accepting the job would guarantee lots of upheaval. I'd be moving back to the place of my birth, for the first time in more than fifty years. I was leaving a considerable amount of money on the table at EA, in the form of equity grants that would vest in the coming years.

For Debbie, who had two kids in high school, it would mean an even greater and more wrenching change. But by then, I couldn't imagine taking the step without Debbie. I had just found my soulmate and myself once again; I wasn't going to lose that now.

It was a crucial period for her kids—Remy was about to start his senior year in high school and Brody was about to become a freshman. But she was game, saying to me at one point, "I want to be wherever you are."

Mum was the word at the time, but I knew I wanted to tell my family. Debbie and I flew to Liverpool later that month for what would turn out to be a grim nil-nil draw with Manchester United. The night before, Debbie and I had dinner at the Titanic Hotel in Liverpool with my siblings and their spouses. I'd told them all about Debbie but this was their first chance to meet her in person. The connection was instant and obvious and we had a brilliant night telling stories.

I saved the last detail for the dessert course. Looking round the table at my siblings, I said, "There's one other thing I wanted you all to know: Debbie and I are moving back to Liverpool in the spring. Because I'm going to be the CEO of Liverpool Football Club."

There was an instant of stunned silence and then a fandango of laughter and cheers. My dear sister Emma literally fell out of her chair. They were all sworn to secrecy until Liverpool made the announcement, which was planned for April, by which time I was due some vesting benefits at EA, and Liverpool could announce the transition right before the end of the campaign.

That plan was moving along smoothly until the morning of February 27, 2017. I got a phone call painfully early in the morning from Mike Gordon. *The Sun*—the Fleet

Street tabloid that had behaved most unscrupulously during the aftermath of the Hillsborough disaster—had gotten the scoop that I was going to be the new CEO at Liverpool, and they were going to go with it in the next day's edition.

We agreed we had to get it out ahead of that. I knew that meant I had to call Andrew Wilson immediately. He was the Section 16 officer, and as a publicly traded company, EA had to publicly announce the move by the end of the business day.

I reached Andrew on the phone early that morning. "I need to talk with you," I said.

"I'm actually having a business breakfast," he said. "Can it wait until this afternoon?"

"I'm sorry, but it really can't," I explained. "I need to let you know that I'm leaving EA."

There was a long pause. "I'm sorry to hear that," he said. "Can I ask where you're going?"

"I'm going to be the CEO of Liverpool Football Club."

There was a further beat of silence, and then Andrew said, his voice cracking, "Mate, I couldn't be happier for you."

Both EA and LFC made the announcement, and then Debbie and I put our heads together, and prepared for the great adventure.

It was time to start a new life ... by going home.

CHAPTER TWELVE

FOLLOW THAT DREAM

Let me say from the outset that getting your dream job of a lifetime is a wonderful thing. But this was more than that. After fifty-plus years of passionately supporting Liverpool FC, I was suddenly in a position of representing the club for a living, and being able to do more than just vociferously cheering for the Reds. This was an opportunity to give back to the club that had provided so much joy to multiple generations in my family. To the city that had given me the Power of Scouseness (watch my TED talk), and to the innumerable people who had given me a helping hand along the way in my career, to whom I would be forever grateful, as none of us are successful without the support of others.

But back to the cheering ... it was the one part that became more difficult. The accepted etiquette in the directors' boxes—where club executives watch separated by just a few feet from their opposing counterparts—demanded a certain degree of protocol. When your team scored you could stand and applaud, but high-fives, fist-bumping, and chants were frowned upon. Even more primal reactions, like yelling that the referee was a "blind Manc t***," were now completely out of the question, even on those occasions when it seemed to be true.

So I found myself back on Merseyside, more than a half-century after my father moved us out of my hometown. On my frequent trips back I'd been in awe of how Liverpool had been transformed, but now I was in the heart of the city, and witnessing that rebirth on a daily basis. Liverpool was bustling, diverse, and forward-looking, though you could still feel the history of the place—the Royal Albert Docks, the Western Approaches (the underground bunker beneath a nondescript building that was the nerve center of the Allies' Atlantic campaign during World War II), even Mathew Street, where the Beatles first made their mark.

By the time I arrived in the spring of 2017, it was becoming clear that, whatever its initial missteps, John Henry's Fenway Sports Group had done a commendable job with Liverpool FC, rescuing the club from the disastrous regime of Americans Tom Hicks and George Gillett (known as "The Cowboys" to disillusioned supporters), navigating through a difficult early learning curve, and eventually settling on a formula that was proving successful.

After hiring the much-coveted Jürgen Klopp in 2015, the club made a series of signings under sporting director Michael Edwards and the scouting staff that yielded an encouragingly high percentage of successful acquisitions. To the eternal credit of John Henry and FSG every bit of revenue the club realized was poured back into the club, for player recruitment and capital improvements like the expanded Main Stand and Megastore at Anfield, and ultimately the new training facility at Kirkby.

If FSG had a shortcoming, it was in the way it connected with the community, or failed to do so. Part of the problem was trying to graft American sports "franchise" sensibilities onto a club steeped in 125 years of tradition. Henry and the Americans were not initially prepared for the depth of commitment between the city's supporters and the club—the notion of supporters having any kind of say in the club's policy was literally foreign to the American executives. A mass walkout in the 77th minute of a match to protest rising ticket prices had smacked FSG in the face in 2016. Thus, despite its successes and its global reach, the club's management was still viewed with suspicion and distrust by many locals.

Our cross-town rival Everton, with a fraction of LFC's revenue, reputation, and resources, still managed to have a more substantial impact with its Everton in the Community organization than we did with the Liverpool FC Foundation. My belief was that I had been hired, in part, to bridge the gap between the owners and the supporters. As a lifelong Liverpool supporter and a boardroom season ticket holder, I understood LFC's rich and complicated history, and possessed the institutional memory that had sometimes been missing in FSG's interaction with supporters.

I had been back in the city for a week or two when I received an invitation to meet the gaffer. Jürgen Klopp and his wife Ulla lived in Formby and asked me around to get acquainted. It was a gesture consistent with the generosity of spirit that Klopp brought to every endeavor. We met at the Klopps' home, then strolled to his local, the Freshfield, a proper pub with more than a dozen different ales on tap.

I sat for three hours with Jürgen, Ulla, and the assistant coach Peter Krawietz. It was a chance for Jürgen to get to know me, and I appreciated the effort, especially since in the main the business side was completely separate from the football side. During the relaxed, rambling conversation, I was struck by the physical magnetism of Klopp. He filled a room up with his presence, without ever calling attention to himself. (And for their part, the neighbors and regulars at the bar greeted him when he arrived then left him alone, as one would hope and expect.)

It was a marvelous night; I thanked him for all he'd done for the club, and vowed I'd do everything in my power to support him from the business side, in an effort to generate revenues that would allow him to bring in even more talent. In talking about how grateful I was, I fear I may have left Jürgen with the impression that my fandom outweighed my business experience and acumen. One of the themes that would emerge in the months and years ahead was me striving to continually prove to my employers that I was a shrewd businessman with a vision for the club that would help it prosper in the future, not just a diehard supporter who happened to have some incidental experience in business. It became a sticking point—I believed that my Liverpool roots and my lifelong support of the club, going back to the late '50s, were an asset, rather than something that blurred my decision making or made me any less effective as the CEO.

•

That summer of 2017, Debbie and I set up in temporary accommodation on the 36th floor of West Tower, the tallest building in Liverpool, right on the waterfront. The skyscraper also housed Panoramic 34, a spectacular restaurant offering 360-degree views out onto the city. It was a perfect place to entertain, and the proprietors Hugh and Cathy Frost became friends (and, eventually, sold us their home on the Wirral, just across the River Mersey).

West Tower was ideally situated, allowing me to reacquaint myself with the rhythms of modern Liverpool, now much more cosmopolitan than the city I'd left. In 2008, it had been named one of the European Capitals of Culture, and began updating its image from, in the words of one analyst, the "very dated images of the city, which ranged from positive but fixed associations with the Beatles in the 1960s to more negative views of social deprivation in the 1980s."

The club's business offices were a seven-minute walk down to Chapel Street, with a beautiful view of the Liver Building and across the Mersey. As the 16/17 season wound down, I listened and observed and asked lots of questions. Like all fans, I sweated through the end of the campaign, with

Liverpool needing a win over Middlesbrough on the final day of the season to clinch qualification in the Champions League.

As I settled into my new job, I soon realized that some of my methods didn't translate as smoothly as I'd hoped. One of my favored tools at EA was my busy Twitter timeline, which I used to strategically engage with gamers, and to put a human face on the company. I had hoped to do the same at Liverpool, but it became apparent that engaging with supporters via the socials was viewed as a bit of a nuisance by my new employers. Liverpool's big summer 2017 signing was the exciting forward Mohamed Salah, signed from Roma. On the June afternoon when Salah visited Anfield, I got a call from our comms department that there was no one at Anfield to greet him, as the manager and the rest of the staff were all on vacation. I said I'd drive over to Anfield to greet Salah, just out of courtesy and so he could receive an official welcome. We chatted, took some pictures, and I posted one on Twitter, of me pointing out across the Anfield pitch, with the facetious caption, "and as you go screaming down the left wing towards the away fans in the Annie Road end, with Bobby and Phil trying to keep up with you..."

Well I got the wing wrong, and the joke fell flat with Boston; clearly someone perceived that I was somehow trying to crowd my way into "football" matters. A couple months later, on the last day of the transfer window, I took a picture of a worker outside my office window on Chapel Street, peering in. He was actually just fixing the cladding on the exterior of the building, but I couldn't resist posting the picture to Twitter, with the caption, "I know everyone is interested in what is happening today, but this is ridiculous." Sky Sports ran it on their transfer day special, and it got thousands of likes. My goal was to add a touch of Scouse humor and a sense of irreverence to the proceedings. Suffice it to say that this objective was not shared by my employers back in Boston, who described the posts as "unstatesmanlike." I reluctantly saw their point, though at the time I was keen to build a stronger relationship with our local supporter base, the people who would stop me on the streets of Liverpool and provide me with their "advice" on how the club should be run.

What I focused on in my first months on the job was finding out where I could carve out a role as the "svelte CEO," as it was described in the interview process. I was dealing with something of a blank slate, because so little of my job was articulated in the job description. Ultimately, I determined that I should focus on the four "C"s—the tentpoles around which I felt the club needed to grow and thrive: *Community*, *Culture*, *Commercial*, and *Civic*. In June, we held a town hall for the club staff—nearly 800 people by this point—at Camp & Furnace, in the heart of the Baltic Triangle. I spoke of my love for the club and my hometown, and elaborated on my mission as I saw it, to strengthen the connection between the club and the city it represented, while expanding the growing number of Liverpool supporters around the globe. It was this mindset that led to the guiding mantra of "Local Heart, Global Pulse."

◆

My first league game in my official capacity as Liverpool CEO was away to Watford in August. The team always traveled to away games the day before, and on this occasion we were staying at a smallish London area hotel. On the night before the opener, I was in the hotel restaurant with club doctor Andy Massey and the team physio Andy Renshaw. We were greeted effusively by the restaurant's assistant manager, who made it a point to tell us how much he appreciated Liverpool staying in the hotel. Later in the evening he came back to our table, holding an old black-and-white photograph and said to me, "It would be an honor for me if you signed this picture for me, Mr. Grobbelaar."

While my dinner companions were stifling their snickers, I tried to figure out the best way to handle the situation. I didn't want to embarrass the gentleman by explaining that, though we shared receding hairlines, I was not the legendary Liverpool keeper Bruce Grobbelaar. So instead I thanked him, borrowed his Sharpie, and concentrated intently while trying to remember how to spell Grobbelaar's last name.

On other occasions, it was clear that there were occupational hazards to being *correctly* identified. Later that fall, Liverpool went to Spurs and were thrashed 5–1, with Jürgen taking off Dejan Lovren after 29 minutes, because he was being utterly abused by Harry Kane. After flying back to Liverpool that night, still wearing my club tie and blazer, I made the mistake of walking downtown to get dinner. A drunk, surly supporter and his mates recognized me, and shouted "Hey, soft arse!," which is never the prelude to an exchange of pleasantries in Liverpool. He came up from behind, grabbing me by the scruff of the neck, then punched me on the back of the head. Zara Dyer, my executive assistant at the time, stepped in before I did something that I might later have regretted, and the man and his crew staggered off. There was a lesson here: It didn't really pay to make yourself visible on those occasions when much of the city was disappointed in the club. Rarely after that did I venture into the city after a match, win, lose, or draw. Lesson well and truly learned.

All part of learning the job. I made an impact where I could. Gamedays at Anfield were obviously the highlight of the rhythm of the work week, and I believed in a tight dress code in the boardroom, where Liverpool FC and their legends entertained visiting club executives and VIPs. I made a point of grabbing the microphone about twenty minutes before kickoff to deliver a few words of welcome to the hundred or so people in the boardroom lounge, always mentioning the visiting executives by name, as well as the legends from the club—Dalglish, Barnes, Rush, and the like—and any visiting VIPs. I felt that was the Liverpool way—we are city of welcoming open arms, and I believed that should be reflected in the way we hosted our opponents, before combat commenced outside on the green battlefield.

It soon became abundantly clear to me that this was a seven-days-a-week role, involved not only in the daily operations of the club, but also representing LFC at various civic, philanthropic, academic, and commercial events, all of which—because of my pride in the club's role in the community—I thoroughly enjoyed, seeing it as part of the CEO's job requirements.

Meanwhile, Debbie took to her new surroundings adroitly. Her immediate comment (and her adoption of the local parlance) held true: "I love the people, even though I can't understand half of what they're saying, but the weather is absolutely shite." Once a California girl, always a California girl. But owing to her quick wit and immense social skills, Debbie moved seamlessly into the role of my wing woman, welcoming visitors, working the room to make sure everyone felt included, presiding over festivities as the perfect co-host. Before one match with a fierce rival, she was entertaining visiting executives while I was making the rounds to greet corporate partners and visitors in other boxes.

I came back to the boardroom and asked her how it was going.

"Yeah," she said smiling. "I just had a lovely chat about wine with a man named Alex."

"Alex?"

"Yeah, nice Scottish gentleman."

I looked at her blankly for a second and then looked over to the corner where the visiting club dignitaries were.

I looked back at Debbie. "Babe," I said, "that was *Sir Alex Ferguson.*"

Debbie is a sommelier by training, and had hit it off with Manchester United's legendary manager, an oenophile in his own right.

Debbie, also a trained yoga teacher, soon began working with the Liverpool FC community team Red Neighbours, directing a chair yoga class for elderly women in the L4, L5, and L6 postcodes near the stadium. Social isolation is a real issue among the elderly, and bringing everyone into the stadium once a week to mingle and do some light exercise proved amazingly popular.

After the first few months living back in Liverpool, it was evident to me how fortunate I had been to be born a Scouser, and everything that came with that that had subsequently helped me in my life and career in the USA. As such, Debbie and I decided to create the Peter Moore Foundation, a charity that we funded from our savings, as a vehicle to give something back to the city that had set me on my way and was always there for me when I had returned over the years. Our initial focus was supporting institutions such as Alder Hey Children's Hospital, where my mum had been a young nurse after World War II, and the Clatterbridge Cancer Centre, helping to fight this insidious disease that affected 50 percent of the population of Merseyside.

Football is a powerful platform through which to deliver social messages. Early on in my tenure, I met the enterprising Ian Byrne (a lifelong Red who belonged to the Spirit of Shankly supporters' group) and Dave Kelly (a lifelong Blue who belonged to Everton's Blue Union supporters' group). They had formed a collective between the two clubs' supporters, soliciting donations for families facing food poverty. I made sure we worked to spread the word about the good work they were doing. Soon the pre-match trip to Tesco to pick up groceries for the cause became a part of the gameday routine of thousands of supporters.

One of the first initiatives of the Peter Moore Foundation was to supply Ian and Dave with a purpose-built van—replacing a groaning old green van they'd been subsisting on—that would go to Anfield for Liverpool home matches and Goodison for Everton home matches. Naturally, it couldn't be painted either red or blue, so combining the two we painted it purple, and worked with Red Neighbours to raise awareness.

◆

Back on the pitch, reinforcements were coming. The summer of 2017 saw the protracted drama of Liverpool's courting of Southampton's stellar center back Virgil van Dijk. In June, the club issued a public apology, ending any formal interest in the player. The day after that public apology, I stopped in Starbucks on my way to the office. As I was leaving, with a Venti Latte in hand, I was spotted by a young lad across the street who shouted, in a thick Scouse accent, "Oi! Baldy! Instead of buying fucking Starbucks, you should've bought fucking van Dijk!" I burst out laughing, glad to be well and truly back home.

The saga ended happily. By January 2018, Virgil had been brought over for a record fee. Signing van Dijk was immense, as he settled down the backline of the defense (to say nothing of supporters' nerves whenever Liverpool had to defend a corner kick). There were still frantic matches—the 4–3 home win in January 2018 over Manchester City, previously unbeaten in the league—but as van Dijk grew more comfortable in the side, you saw Liverpool mature in front of your eyes.

And as we moved through the Round of 16 in the Champions League campaign, it was becoming apparent

Clockwise from left: my parents on their wedding day at St. George's Hall in Liverpool; me at age one, in Hurstlyn Road; my dad and mum with me, Andy, and baby Phil in the Gay Cavalier, circa 1962

Clockwise from top: Terry Moore in his element, behind the bar at the Red Lion; me and Andy, nearly Irish twins; on my tricycle in Garston, Liverpool (unclear why I'm not wearing any pants...)

Opposite page, top to bottom: Yale High School football team picture, Welsh National School Champions (I'm in the back row, third from left; Chris Marsden front row, third from left; O.M. Edwards, front row, far right); Ysgol Dinas Bran, 1981 (I'm in the blue tracksuit on the far left), with the young Welsh farmers' lads I molded into a rugby team; Terry Moore and his kids, from left, Andy, Phil, Emma, and me, at a time when all the men in the family had dodgy mustaches

DINAS BRAN
SCHOOL
1980-81
Mitre

Clockwise from top: me in Munich, in one of our trusty Patrick vans; Bernice, me, Tara, and Tyler, northern California, 1987; Reebok's 1996 Liverpool FC kit launch, with LFC CEO Peter Robinson; testifying in the Senate on behalf of the video-game industry, 2002 (image courtesy of CSPAN network)

Clockwise from top: Bill Gates looking on as I extol the virtues of the Xbox 360; showing Steven Spielberg around the Xbox booth at E3 in 2005; the portrayal of EA's infamous president "Mr. Peters," with the *South Park* boys (used with permission by Comedy Central © 2025 Paramount Media Networks); with David Beckham at the launch of EA Sports Active, Los Angeles, 2009

From top to bottom: welcoming the Egyptian King Mo Salah to Anfield in the summer of 2017; celebrating LFC's World Club Cup championship with Jürgen Klopp and Billy Hogan in Doha, December 2019; with the light of my life: Debbie and me on our wedding day in Liverpool, August 2018

From top to bottom: Virgil and me with "Big Ears," Madrid 2019 (photo credit: John Powell/LFC); with Sir Kenny Dalglish and Ian Rush, sharing the joy of being crowned Premier League champions, tinged with the sadness of not being able to share the moment with supporters; the one we wanted for so many years, with the Premier League trophy at Anfield, summer 2020 (photo credit: Andy Powell/LFC)

From top to bottom: the blended family, all together on the Serengeti: from left to right, Tara, Remy, Brodie, Debbie, me, Alex, Toni-Marie, Angela, and Tyler; football is life and comes full circle, as Wrexham visit Santa Barbara for a pre-season friendly, July 2024

that under Klopp, we could compete with anyone. After smashing Porto in the Round of 16, we were disappointed to be drawn against a domestic rival—tournament favorites Manchester City—in the Champions League quarterfinal, but one also got the sense that we were ready to test ourselves against the very best.

Jürgen Klopp and Pep Guardiola genuinely liked and respected each other, so there would be none of the Ferguson/Wenger mind games that had become such a part of English football. But for all the excitement surrounding the first leg of the tie, to be played at Anfield, there was also concern. With the extensive construction going on in the approach to the stadium on Anfield Road, the access point for the team coaches' arrival would be choked. By then, we'd routinely see thousands of supporters lining up on Anfield Road to greet Liverpool. Given the stakes, and the intense rivalry with any team that begins with the word Manchester, it was obvious that Anfield Road would be a hostile gauntlet for City's coach to go through.

Out of an excess of caution, we consulted with my friend Andy Cooke, the chief constable of Merseyside and his experienced matchday operations team. We suggested to the City executives that the club could avoid the crowds by going a different route, parking by the Sir Kenny Dalglish Stand, and then walking around the perimeter of the field to the dressing rooms. But word came back that the team didn't want to take anything but a direct route to the dressing room access doors under the Main Stand.

So we hired extra security, knowing all the while that we were tempting fate. That afternoon the crowds built and built, in a raucous, festive mood. As the Manchester City coach came through, it was greeted with a volley of flares and, eventually, projectiles—bottles, rocks, even a brick or two. Once the coach finally got into the secure area, with its windscreen cracked, Pep Guardiola got off first, offering a tight-lipped, sarcastic, "Thanks for the protection" to the gameday staff. The City executives had come in a Mercedes just behind the coach and as soon as they arrived in the boardroom, I went over to apologize for the incident.

Two things were true: The behavior was completely unacceptable, and the handful of Liverpool supporters who threw things at the bus were not behaving in the best interests of themselves or the club. We've spent decades trying to undo those old stereotypes. UEFA fined the club for the ugly incident.

And/but... On the night, after that experience and in front of an Anfield crowd that was incandescent, City were clearly rattled. Whether that was anything to do with the hostile greeting upon arrival, who knows, but the Mighty Reds were irresistible that night, scoring three goals in a 20-minute first-half stretch, with a magnificent Alex Oxlade-Chamberlain strike from distance a key part of the onslaught.

Two weeks later, on the occasion of the second leg of the quarterfinal, we drove to Manchester, to the Etihad Stadium, gleaming antiseptic home to the Cityzens. City were putting on a good face, and rightly believed they had the talent and tactical discipline to overturn the deficit. To fire up their sometimes muted fanbase, the club had outfitted the stadium with 60,000 tiny white and sky blue plastic flags in every seat.

A half-hour before kickoff, I was seated with Kenny Dalglish, looking out on the scene in the Liverpool visitors' box. Kenny surveyed the assembled throng, as they were holding their little pennants aloft, and said, "Do they realize they're all waving white flags? Bunch of ninnies." City roused their fans with an early goal, but this Liverpool side was full of character and resolve. The Reds equalized and eventually won the game outright, 2–1, to advance to the Champions League semifinal. Did Kenny celebrate a bit more vociferously than was the custom in the directors' box when those two goals went in? Yes. Were our City hosts glaring at us? Also yes, and I'd never loved him more.

Then it was on to the semifinal against Roma, where the first leg was again at Anfield. It was just a few minutes into the game when I received a tap on my shoulder, from Andy Hughes, the club's chief operating officer. If it's true that as a manager, you never want a call at 3 in the morning, because it's always going to be because something's going wrong, it's also true that, as a club CEO, any interruption during the match inevitably means that there has been a problem in and around the ground.

In this case, it was outside the stadium, on Walton Breck Road, close to the Albert Pub. An Irish Liverpool supporter had been ambushed by a few balaclava-clad Roma ultras, cowardly thugs who knocked him down, beat him badly with a belt buckle, and then scampered off before they could be apprehended. The fan, a Dunboyne family man named Sean Cox, had been rushed to Aintree Medical Center, and it wasn't clear whether he was going to make it.

The club's crisis management team had already sprung into action, working with Merseyside Police to get access to CCTV footage from outside the pub. Meanwhile, investigators began combing the area looking for leads. A kindly old lady reported that she'd seen one assailant run down the alley, throw his sweatshirt in the trash, replacing it with a different one, and then set off to the stadium. With the positive ID from the woman about what the ultra was wearing into the stadium, undercover police officers went into the Roma crowd and found the assailants and extricated them during the match. It was a heroic bit of crisis-management policing, but it did little for Sean Cox, who wound up in a coma.

While the attack had occurred outside of the stadium perimeter, I knew that Liverpool FC wanted to do everything it could to help. All three of Cox's assailants eventually served prison time, but the medical costs for Cox would run to millions of euros. We supported a GoFundMe page for Sean, and later I met with his wife, Martina, and Liverpool pledged its support so that Sean would be taken care of for the rest of his life.

It was around this time that I was reminded of the scope of Liverpool's support, from the city out to Ireland and Europe and the rest of the world. We took every precaution we could for the second leg, at Roma, wanting to make sure there was no further trouble. That was a wild game, finishing with two late goals by Roma that made the tie much closer than we wanted, but we emerged 7–6 winners in the tie. The players brought out a banner honoring Sean Cox for the post-match celebration. He was never far from our thoughts during that and subsequent seasons, as his amazing family focused on getting him home, establishing a new normal for a man whose life would be forever changed because of the despicable actions of a handful of so-called fans who have served their time and are now back home in Italy

Shortly after the emotional high of clinching the tie in Roma, we came upon the harsh practical realities of planning transportation for our team, staff, and supporters to the Champions League final, scheduled that year for Kyiv. It instantly became apparent that it was going to be difficult as hell to even *get* to Kyiv. The airport runways weren't long enough for bigger planes, and there wasn't enough space in the airport to charter as many as would be required. Suddenly thousands of people were faced with finding alternate routes. We were 1,700 miles away from Kyiv, but this wasn't like flying from New York to LA. It was much more like trying to get from New York to, say, Boise, Idaho. Many wound up driving, and some of our staff had to take a 38-hour bus ride to make it to Kyiv.

But Scousers get where water can't, and when we arrived, the streets were bouncing, and there were Liverpool fans everywhere, congregating for the club's first Champions League final in 11 seasons. Estimates ranged from 10,000 to 20,000, and many if not most didn't even have tickets to the match. At Shevchenko Plaza, they partied, and Liverpool's own Jamie Webster led one of the Boss Nights.

The morning of the final, Debbie and I were given a tour of Kyiv, and were struck by the beautiful city with its sad history. The tour guide took us to Babyn Yar, where 33,000 Jews were killed by the Nazi SS *Einsatzgruppen* during the war—and more were killed by the Soviets after the war.

When the match finally started, one couldn't help but sense that this young Liverpool team were still a bit naïve. We were certainly unfortunate. The dark arts that led Sergio Ramos to pin Mo Salah's arm while bringing him down cost us the sensation of the season, and took away our momentum. Even after Sadio Mane's goal equalized in the 55th minute, we didn't seem to fully have our sea legs. Then the ball that went through Loris Karius's hands for a howler, before Gareth Bale's second goal, a proper worldie, sealed the deal. The final score was 3–1.

Losing a Champions League final is devastating. That night in Kyiv, we went back to the hotel and shared a drink with other staff and our corporate partners. It was a muted postmortem, made all the more difficult by the flukiness of the first Bale goal, and concerns about Salah, who instantly became a doubt for that summer's World Cup.

The next morning, after we arrived back in Liverpool, I saw a video making the rounds. It was made early morning after the final, after it looked as though Jürgen Klopp had imbibed several bottles of beer. There he was, with assistant coach Peter Krawietz, his longtime buddy Campino, from the German pop-rock band Die Titen Hosen, and the German TV host/journalist Johannes B. Kerner, and the four were bouncing arm in arm, singing a ditty they'd composed on the spot:

We saw the European Cup
Madrid had all the fuckin' luck
We swear we'll keep on being cool
We'll bring it BACK TO LIV-ER-POOL!

All around the world, Scousers—and Scousers in spirit—were recovering from the disappointment, and Jürgen's video was just the tonic. The message was clear: Football remained "the most important of the least important things," and so he wasn't going to go into hiding just because the Reds lost a football match. At the same time, the season was a marker that Liverpool had laid down: the Mighty Reds were back.

CHAPTER THIRTEEN

THE VIRTUOUS CYCLE

Even from a distance, you could feel the momentum building. At the end of the 2016/17 season, I traveled with the team for a postseason friendly in Sydney, Australia. The 72,000 in attendance had serenaded the team with one of the more rousing, spine-tingling versions of "You'll Never Walk Alone." By then, there were over 300 Official Liverpool Supporters Club chapters in 100 countries around the world. In a three-year span, I managed to visit in person and speak to 16 different chapters, from Hong Kong to Austin, Singapore to Cape Town, Bangkok to Dubai.

Those visits were emphatic reminders that Liverpool's local heart possessed an unmistakably global pulse. Of course, LFC had for decades been one of the most decorated clubs in all of football, but it had started to decline in the early '90s, precisely when the Premier League separated itself from the Football League and went global. Under Klopp, Liverpool had reasserted itself as a club with one of the largest and most enthusiastic fanbases in the world.

That worldwide interest meant that the increasingly cosmopolitan Liverpool was getting visitors from all over the world. I remember a friend telling me about a taxi ride he took in Liverpool. "When Liverpool play," his Afghani cab driver explained, "we have people from Japan, Australia, US, Germany, Nigeria, *everywhere* in the city. When Everton play, it's just like any other day."

With the demand for tickets at Anfield being so strong, some locals felt they were being squeezed out. In some circles there was a building resentment of the success, a feeling that the team had become *too* international. In my public talks—and it seemed I was talking to some organization somewhere on an almost daily basis—I made the point that both the local and global elements were essential. Liverpool FC had risen to international fame on the back of its supporters, the Liverpudlians who through their enthusiasm, loyalty, and distinctly Scouse spirit and humor provided the club with an unmistakable identity. This was one of the club's great strengths.

But change was inevitable. In the modern wired world, a club truly needed worldwide revenue to compete for the largest prizes. That's why the global following and the revenue it provided was critical. The same held true with on-field talent. You couldn't have—and wouldn't want—11 white British males walking onto the field to be cheered by 50,000 other white British males.

The Liverpool team that Klopp had assembled offered a splendid mix of styles and also nationalities, with the "Fab Three" front line led by the Egyptian icon Mo Salah, the world-class Senegalese Sadio Mane (both were Muslim), and the tireless Brazilian Roberto Firmino, with the erudite Belgian Divock Origi providing decisive goals off the bench.

The midfield was paced by the English pair of Jordan Henderson and the veteran James Milner, but included key cogs like the influential No. 6, the Brazilian Fabinho; the versatile Dutch workhorse Gini Wijnaldum; the Guinean talent Naby Keita; and the Swiss "PowerCube," Xherdan Shaqiri.

The back line of defense was anchored by the majestic Virgil van Dijk, pairing with the Cameroonian Joel Matip (as well as the fleet but injury-prone English central defender Joe Gomez), and the young Scouser in the team, Trent Alexander-Arnold, haring down the right side, with the scrappy Scottish star Andy Robertson patrolling the left. The summer signing of Brazilian Alisson brought the exemplary goalkeeping we needed, the last crucial element in Klopp's team-building.

There's one other thing worth mentioning, especially at a time when so many trolls complain about spoiled, overpaid athletes. This collection of absolute superstars also comprised the most impressive group of human beings I've ever had the privilege of being around. They were professional, patient, courteous, and wholly dedicated to their craft, their club and each other. I've been around a lot of teams in my life, both athletic and corporate, and this was a rare, exceptional group. A lot of that is down to the men themselves, but the *esprit de corps* was instilled by Jürgen and his staff, and was one of the key elements in the success we enjoyed during this period.

Both Salah and Mane would kiss the ground after scoring, less in prayer than to give thanks, they explained. At a time when the Tory government was turning immigration into a wedge issue, Klopp's Liverpool offered a counter perspective on the strength of diversity. And that positive example made a difference. A Stanford University Immigration Policy Lab study reported that since the arrival of Salah, hate crimes in and around Liverpool went down by nearly 20 percent, and anti-Muslim comments were reduced by 50 percent.

One couldn't help but notice the virtuous cycle that was emerging. Under Klopp, Liverpool's fortunes improved dramatically, which brought more interest from fans, media, and sponsors. On the business side, we strove to present a more accessible, more human face to our supporters, and moved aggressively to augment our revenue from corporate partners. That increased revenue was then poured back into the club for acquisitions and upgrades.

It was a special time for the football club, with Liverpool experiencing a renaissance competitively, aesthetically, and financially. I wanted to make sure we were doing all we could to serve Jürgen, the coaching staff, the medical and nutritional staff, and the players on the pitch.

I also wanted to get everyone pulling in the same direction on the business side. That compelled me to compose a club-wide manifesto, which I'd done before at EA Sports. I remember staying up late one night, a glass of red wine at my side for inspiration and clarity. I came up with the following credo, introduced at a town hall meeting and distributed to everyone on the business side:

"We are Liverpool. We hold our heads high, and have always stood together through the wind and the rain. We exist to achieve success and realise our fans' dreams. Without their belief we would be nothing. As one team, we have a duty to build Liverpool to the pinnacle and set the standards for all to follow.

"We are caring neighbours in this unique city; we always give back while inspiring and nurturing those in need. Our pulse is global, our heart is local, and You'll Never Walk Alone is both our anthem and our rallying cry. And above all, we live by the values and the unique code we call The Liverpool Way."

A vast majority of our staff embraced it, though in some corners I noticed a little bit of the classic British reserve of folded arms and clenched jaw—it all seemed a bit *too* American for some people. I would learn that this wasn't something that was routinely done in British corporate culture. I persevered, though. I believed it was important to define what we were about, and what we were trying to accomplish.

Also, I wanted to set a standard that we would each hold ourselves to. I remembered how grim things got in the Hicks and Gillett days, when supporters felt the people running the club didn't care about the very people who were responsible for Liverpool becoming such a revered entity in the first place.

At heart, the manifesto plugged into a belief that FSG's actions already supported. They weren't "owners" and this wasn't a "franchise." We were caretakers of a football club that was also, to a greater degree than almost any other club in the world, a public trust. We had to be mindful of their interests.

Publicly, the connection was underscored by the *We Are Liverpool: This Means More* campaign launched earlier that spring. The Liverpool club historian Mark Platt and video producer Phil Reade helped develop the campaign, culminating in a brilliant spot that clocked in at just under two minutes. "For others it's a sport, for us it's a way of life. They have a stadium; we have a home. They have songs; we have anthems." Originally, the voiceover was done by a narrator with a Scouse accent. But then they tried it with Jürgen Klopp doing the voiceover, and it was perfect. It had been introduced to support New Balance's kit rollout, but it endured far beyond that.

The slogan itself drove many of our rivals and rival supporters batshit crazy, and I gathered that they may have found it particularly maddening because it was all kind of true. We had the best supporters, we had the best anthem, we had the best gameday environment. Speaking of the atmosphere at Anfield, even Pep Guardiola admitted, "There is something about it that you will find in no other stadium in the world."

The team's success only increased the fanaticism of the response. The club was becoming so successful, in fact, that when I would go around the world to talk to supporters' clubs, the question I would most often hear was, "Why can't we find the Liverpool gear anywhere?" New Balance had come up with some unique, sophisticated kits, but demand outpaced supply, sometimes to ridiculous proportions. In the grand scheme of problems, this was a good one to have.

The start of the 2018/19 season also coincided with a remarkably happy time in my life. Back in Liverpool, I had been able to reconnect with my family, as all three of my siblings were now successfully married, and still living on the same street in Marford, just around the corner from the Red Lion—which by now had changed hands several times, and had become an Indian restaurant, though it retained its name. Suddenly I had the privilege of spending time with them as adults, getting to know their spouses and their families. My brother Andy had become a huge Liverpool fan, and often made it out to games. Phil worked as a senior officer in the Liverpool police force, and Emma was working as a teacher's assistant.

Late that August—timed to coincide with the eve of the international break, of course—Debbie and I were married. I'd proposed earlier that spring in a crowded restaurant in Rome and we knew we wanted to hold the ceremony sooner rather than later, so August 31 became the date. We'd planned on getting married at our home, Axholme, on the Wirral, until we discovered that you can't legally get married at home in Britain. So that day we went down to St. George's Hall in Liverpool—the same place my mum and dad were wed—to get our marriage certificate, then began a weekend-long celebration. The day emerged bright and sunny, and we'd rented an open-top bus to bring around many of our American friends who'd never seen Liverpool before. The day after the wedding, Liverpool played away at the King Power Stadium, and the Leicester City CEO Susan Whelan graciously let me rent a box for a few dozen visitors to witness. It was a wonderful time, made all the more so by Liverpool's 2–1 win.

◆

That 18/19 season was in so many ways a dream campaign. Going in, the conventional wisdom had held that Liverpool could compete in the domestic cups and even have success in Europe because of the cauldron that was Anfield, but that our club didn't have the finances or the depth to mount a serious season-long title challenge against Manchester City's juggernaut. It was a logical assumption, but Liverpool under Klopp were regularly dispatching logical assumptions. He had built a club which exuded this marrow-deep self-belief on the part of the players. They had begun to realize that on their day, they were as good as any team in the world, and they were willing to fight together to the last second for the badge, for the gaffer, for the supporters, and for each other.

Even when things looked bleakest, Liverpool always seemed to find a way. The hallmark was that December's Merseyside derby at home against Everton. The Toffees came in determined to play a stultifying, negative, time-wasting game characterized by little more than rampant diving and non-stop shithousery. This much they certainly accomplished. They were playing for the nil-nil draw from the first minute and, deep into stoppage time of a chippy match (five yellow cards were issued), it seemed, to their credit, they would get what they wanted. Then came the legendary finish.

If you're a Liverpool fan, you've probably seen the replay a hundred times: In the sixth minute of stoppage time, Alisson pushed the ball across midfield to Trent, who launched it into the mixer, where an Everton defender headed the ball away, toward Virgil van Dijk on the edge of the box. Virgil's mishit volley ballooned into the air and bounced off the crossbar, just out of reach of the Everton keeper Jordan Pickford. By the time it took a second deflection off the bar, the consummate poacher Divock Origi had positioned himself perfectly to head the ball into the goal, while the flailing Pickford tried to comprehend what had just happened.

He wasn't alone. The ball bouncing off the bar produced a collective gasp in the stands before Origi's header prompted a shocked Anfield crowd to explode in a chorus of what could only be described as gleeful astonished joy. Everybody kind of lost their minds for a moment. Jürgen ran onto the pitch for a hug with Alisson (he happily paid the £8,000 fine for entering the pitch during the match).

What I remember best about the aftermath was Bill Kenwright, the Everton chairman, sitting across the aisle from me. Bill, an exceedingly decent man, and as devoted a Blue as ever lived, had seen every Everton calamity going back thirty-five years. At the recognition of what had happened, Bill just buried his head in his hands and sat there, inconsolable, disbelieving for the better part of five minutes after the final whistle. We didn't go anywhere near him out of respect for the pain he was obviously feeling. Football, bloody football. It can provide ejector seat moments of unbridled joy, but at the same time, unfathomable depths of outright despair.

As Liverpool marched through the end of December without a loss, it became clear that they were in the title race for the long haul. City were also excellent, and the two teams' early January battle away was testament to the finest of margins that would decide the race. The Cityzens prevailed 2–1, but only because a Sadio Mane shot was cleared within 11.7 millimeters from crossing the line for a goal.

It was in February of that year that I was invited to Oxford University to speak at one of the most historic and revered platforms for debate and speeches. Since 1823, the Oxford Union has hosted presidents, prime ministers, and a who's who of great thinkers and influencers across politics, science, religion, and the arts. I had spoken to a lot of crowds in a lot of grand and diverse places, but this was one of the few venues that compelled me to pause and consider the distance traveled from my somewhat humble childhood in Liverpool. It was an honor to address the students about Liverpool Football Club and its unique place in sports and society, and the lessons we were learning about the positive social impact that the Beautiful Game could have on literally billions of people around the world.

Through that winter, with the beginning of the Champions League knockout phase and the heart of the title race, Liverpool had become one of the most entertaining teams in the world. Then there was serendipity. Salah continued to rack up goals, and became something more than a star. By now, as the highest-profile athlete from Africa, in the world's most popular sport, he was becoming an international icon. Around the world, you would see videos of scenes of thousands of Liverpool fans staying up late or getting up early to watch Liverpool matches. That spring of 2019, Salah was named one of the 100 most influential people in the world by *Time* magazine and wound up on the cover (looking particularly dashing in our handsome "deep violet" away kit). When *Time* hosted a lavish dinner for the 100 honorees, Jürgen let Mo fly over to New York City to attend. It was not the sort of opportunity that Roger Hunt or Ian St. John would ever have had.

CHAPTER FOURTEEN

NEVER GIVE UP

Throughout that winter and spring of 2019, Liverpool kept winning, and kept marching through the Champions League knockout rounds. After drawing with Bayern at home in the Round of 16, they went to the Allianz Arena in Munich and completely outclassed Bayern, 3–1, with Sadio Mane scoring twice and Virgil van Dijk adding another. The quarterfinal tie began with a 2–0 win at home against Porto, and then was sealed in the return leg in Portugal, with Mane scoring another brace in a 4–1 win.

Our reward for all this was the most daunting challenge of all: a semifinal tie against Barcelona, merely the most glamorous, renowned club in world football.

Traveling on May 1 to the Camp Nou—Europe's largest football stadium—the Reds played marvelously, but Barcelona got every break en route to a 2–0 lead. Lionel Messi's masterful free kick to make it 3–0 felt like a dagger; Alisson had 99 percent of the goal covered, but Messi found the other 1 percent in the top corner. Meanwhile, we were hitting the post and having shots cleared off the line. There was a late Barca breakaway opportunity that could have added more damage, but it was foiled. One couldn't help but be discouraged; we had played reasonably well, and a 3–0 loss was not a scoreline we deserved. Josep Bartomeu, the gregarious Barca chairman, whom I was sitting next to at that match, shook my hand after the final whistle and said, "We were lucky to win by three, but I know it will be a different story at Anfield next week."

In the days ahead, all we had was hope. Faced with the nearly impossible task, Klopp had been frank and reasonable when asked about the prospects of turning over a three-goal deficit against the sublimely talented Barcelona side. "If we can do it, wonderful," he said. "If not, then let's fail in the most beautiful way."

Then there were the injuries. By the morning of the second leg, we knew we'd be without both Mohamed Salah, sidelined after recovering from a concussion in our rugged weekend fixture against Newcastle, as well as his frontline mate Roberto Firmino, who'd suffered a soft-tissue injury in the first leg.

On the afternoon of the second leg back in Liverpool, we took the visiting Barca executives and the delegate from UEFA for what is known as "the Protocol Lunch," at chef Paul Askew's excellent restaurant, the Art School. Paul always created a menu that celebrated the best of local ingredients, and his staff laid on a magnificent dining experience in the private room at the restaurant. I presented a sculpture of the Liver bird—crafted by the celebrated Liverpool artist and great friend Emma Rodgers—to Bartomeu and the Barca delegation.

When conversation turned to the game that night, I pointed out our obvious predicament: With Barcelona holding a 3–0 lead in the tie, and with the away goals rule in play, if they scored just one goal, LFC would need five to beat them.

"I'm worried," Bartomeu said.

"Come on," I said, not entirely believing his sincerity.

"No, I'm worried. You outplayed us last week; I don't know how we won three-nil."

Neither did we. Back at the office, we joked all through the day to ease the tension, conjuring up past miracles from Anfield to Istanbul, and making oblique references to St. Jude—the patron saint of hope and lost causes.

For Debbie and me, the evening began the way most

matchdays did—stopping by Tesco for a couple bags of groceries on the way to Anfield. We arrived near the stadium around 6 p.m., and stopped off at the Fans Supporting Foodbanks van to drop off the groceries.

We were bundled up in coats, as it was unseasonably cold—even for Liverpool—on that evening of May 7. As on every other gameday since becoming Liverpool FC's chief executive officer, I was dressed in the navy-blue club suit with the LFC crest on the blazer, and a red tie, featuring a small silhouette of the Liver bird. Debbie looked glamorous and beautiful as always, in a dark crimson dress and a matching necklace.

At the Fans Supporting Foodbanks van just outside the stadium, I had a brief conversation with Ian Byrne, the devout Liverpool fan and Hillsborough survivor who, along with Evertonian Dave Kelly, had started the food relief effort. Ian's mood was cautiously hopeful—"If we can just get an early goal, then let's see..."—but he also was of a mind that the task before us was probably impossible.

"If we can just get an early goal..." was a line I heard dozens of times in the six days between the two legs of the tie. It was as if we were all speaking into existence a glimmer of hope that still existed in our hearts. At the same time, we knew of the power of Barcelona, led by the living legend Lionel Messi and two former Liverpool stars, Luis Suarez and Philippe Coutinho.

Regardless of the grimness of the outlook, our supporters had shown up in full throat. Outside the ground, they greeted the arrival of the LFC team coach with flares and sustained applause. Inside, they sang the club anthem "You'll Never Walk Alone," and also serenaded the team in warm-ups with our unofficial Champions League song, "Allez Allez Allez."

We've conquered all of Europe, we're never going to stop...

I'd heard the murmur of cheers go up on the field about an hour before kickoff, but had not seen the impetus—Salah in civilian clothes, sporting a T-shirt that read "Never Give Up." We weren't missing only Mo and Bobby Firmino. Midfielders Naby Keita and Adam Lallana were also out, leaving a threadbare lineup that included two green 19-year-olds on the bench. Meanwhile, Barcelona, who had already clinched the La Liga title, had rested all 11 of their starters from the first leg during their weekend fixture.

As Messi and Suarez and Coutinho and company got off the Barca coach and entered Anfield sporting their club-issued bespoke gray suits, they looked like a group of young bankers arriving at a conference on investing. Meanwhile, Jürgen and his team had made their way on the Liverpool team coach from the aptly named Hope Street Hotel where the playing squad and coaches traditionally stayed the night before home matches.

Upstairs in the boardroom, we greeted dignitaries and visitors while awaiting the starting lineups, which came out 90 minutes before kickoff. At the stroke of 6:30, someone asked, "What's Jürgen done, then?" In the question itself was a sign of the trust we'd put in the gaffer. (When supporters don't trust a manager they routinely call him by his surname—such as, "What's Hodgson done now?")

What Jürgen had done was throw the experienced squad player Xherdan Shaqiri and the weekend's heroic substitute, Divock Origi (whose late goal had bested Newcastle and kept us in the torrid Premier League race, just a point off of Manchester City), into the front line with the irrepressible Sadio Mane, and then opted for experience and grit in the midfield—captain Jordan Henderson and veteran vice-captain James Milner in with holding midfielder Fabinho. The back line featured the formidable center back Virgil van Dijk teaming with the reliable Joel Matip, and our two gifted full backs, Andy Robertson and the preternaturally talented Trent Alexander-Arnold.

As the teams walked out in the chilly night, Jürgen was wearing a snood, which he saved for the cold games, and our goalkeeper Alisson was sporting a rarely seen silver kit, a third-choice variation so as not to clash with Barca's highlighter-yellow away strip or the Turkish referee's blue shirt.

We had witnessed sporting miracles before—late winners at Anfield, impossible goals wrenched from impossible circumstances, like St. Etienne in 1977 and Olympiakos in 2004, just for starters. But it was one thing to see Everton's short-armed goalkeeper fail to collect a shanked stoppage-time volley—it was another thing altogether to try to turn over a three-goal deficit against the richest club in football.

The match began at 8 p.m. on this crisp night—a roar greeting the opening whistle—and right away you could sense that the lads and the crowd had arrived with an attitude of indomitability. There was a delicious moment early on that had nothing to do with the run of play, yet set the stage for all that followed: In the first minute, Messi broke down the middle, chased by Andy Robertson. As he approached the Liverpool penalty area, he was dispossessed by a fine slide tackle from Fabinho, then was tumbled over by a chasing Robertson. That left the world's best player sitting on the grass, both arms raised pleading for a foul, even as the action was moving in the opposite direction. Robertson got up and on his way back up the pitch, gave the sitting Messi a quick, harmless two-handed shove on the back of the head, prompting fury from the world's best player and delighted laughter from the stands. The message was clear: This leg of the tie would be different.

The early goal that we'd all been asking for came in the seventh minute, with Mane's one-touch pass finding a marauding Henderson in the box. His low shot was parried by the Barca goalkeeper Marc ter Stegen right into the path of Origi, who slotted home, sending our box and the rest of the stadium into rapture. I snuck a glance to my left at the visiting Barca executives. To say that anxiety was etched on their faces would be an understatement. What had just happened was exactly what they feared, and why Bartomeu had seemed so irrationally concerned at lunch.

The "twelfth man" at Anfield was activated. Bellowing, concussive chants emanating from the stands

Li-ver-pool! [clap-clap-clap]
Li-ver-pool! [clap-clap-clap]
Li-ver-pool! [clap-clap-clap]

This was exactly what we'd hoped for, a goal that could put us within realistic range, needing two more goals to level the tie. But in the directors' box and beyond, we remained keenly aware of living on the knife's edge. From the eleventh minute on there was a period of about ten minutes that felt like utter torture: A Fabinho yellow for a foul on Suarez, a Messi shot heading straight for goal tipped over by Alisson, a scoring opportunity for Jordi Alba squandered with a too-late pass to Messi, and, most unnervingly, a three-on-two with Messi flanked by former LFC stars Coutinho and Suarez, foiled by Alisson's alert diving deflection to the left. When Alisson was on, which was most of the time, he was quite possibly the best goalkeeper in the world. It was clear that it was going to take something special to get by him. The fans were rising with every contested ball, every dispossession, every foiled Barca thrust.

But when you're trying to do the unthinkable, you're vulnerable to any twist of fate. About a half-hour in, our captain Henderson went down with what looked like a serious injury. Our stalwart midfielder Gini Wijnaldum was up and off the bench, ready to come on as a substitute, but Hendo shook it off and indicated he was going to stay. Not five minutes later, Suarez—in a classic bit of the darks arts that he routinely practiced—clattered into Andy Robertson, leaving him limping. Throughout the stadium, the Liverpool faithful stood nervously or, in the directors' box, leaned on the edge of seats, just trying to ride out the half. In first-half stoppage time, Messi launched a rocket that just went wide, and even as we were exhaling, I was assuring everyone around me that "Ali would have had that. I *think*."

Halftimes are different when one is in the directors' box. As the official emissary of LFC, and the nominal host of the evening, it was my policy not to drink anything stronger than hot chocolate during a game. One circulates during the interval, but doesn't talk to the executives from the other club during that break—they routinely retire to their private dining area and confer among themselves. But as I snuck an occasional glance their way, I could tell they were, if not obviously panicked, then at least *concerned.* Our side of the boardroom was a sea of hopeful but nerve-wracked faces, eagerly anticipating a second half kicking toward the Kop, but still mindful that a single goal from Barca would make a rally not merely implausible but virtually impossible.

The Anfield crowd remained in fine form, even at halftime.

> *Bring on your Internazionale, bring on your Roma by the score...*

Then the Reds came out for the second half, accompanied by an announcement that Robertson couldn't continue, and would be replaced by Wijnaldum. This put Wijnaldum in at midfield, and moved the versatile Milner to full back.

There are moments when you're trying to climb the highest mountains when it seems like the performance is there but the breaks may not be with you. I had that thought after a Liverpool corner in the 52nd minute, when Virgil van Dijk cleverly sent a backheel toward goal, only to have the alert ter Stegen make the save.

But we kept at it, the crowd urging the team every step of the way. Then the chain of events started, occurring so quickly that afterward it was hard to comprehend just how Trent Alexander-Arnold stole a pass and then crossed into the box where Wijnaldum pounced and delivered a sweet shot past ter Stegen. Now it was 3–2; game definitely on. As the Anfield crowd erupted, Gini ran into the goal, where ter Stegen was still prone, and wrested the ball out of the keeper's hands, then sprinted back to the center circle to a crescendo of cheers.

As the teams waited for the restart—a routine VAR check—I noticed the Barca stars. Messi was standing still at midfield, looking bewildered, and, yards away from him, Suarez was staring straight ahead but subtly shaking his head back and forth, like he couldn't believe what was happening. That for me was the tell—deep down Suarez understood the danger Barca were in, because he'd been here before, and witnessed what a cauldron Anfield could be.

The noise by now seemed a palpable, physical thing. Liverpool quickly retook possession and found Origi down the right channel. His cross went beyond Shaqiri, who rallied to regain possession and passed back to Milner, who dribbled forward and returned it to Shaqiri. Just like that, the Swiss "PowerCube" crossed in front of goal where Wijnaldum—that man again—headed the ball into the net, sending the assembled masses on the Kop into rapture. Two minutes earlier, we were working on a dream. Suddenly, just that quickly, we were living it.

The crowd was giddy, and in the directors' box I heard Ian Rush and Kenny Dalglish, sitting side by side, animatedly reveling in one of those rare, exceptional moments that they'd not only witnessed in the past but also helped create. Meanwhile, the crowd had become this surging, seething presence.

When the Reds ... go marching in ... oh, when the Reds go marching in...

The two teams—each now finely taut, realizing the next goal could be decisive—battled back and forth, though very little of consequence happened over the next twenty minutes. Then another Alexander-Arnold steal led to a Liverpool threat, the ball recycling back to Trent coming down the right wing. He juked and paused, juked again and earned a corner kick.

What happened in the following seconds was so simple and so indelible. The ballboy—soon-to-be folk hero Oakley William Cannonier—hurried a ball to Trent, while fielding the ball that had bounced onto the pitch. Trent placed the ball in the corner and started walking toward the advancing Shaqiri, as if they'd decided on a specific set piece that Shaqiri would take. But suddenly Trent turned back around to the corner and struck the ball. *"Corner taken quickly..."*

Barca had switched off but the alert Divock Origi—as surprised as anyone else to see the ball coming his way—had the presence of mind to take it out of the air on the bounce and redirect it goalward. A second earlier ter Stegen and another Barca defender had realized the ball was in play, but by the time they moved to contest the shot, Origi had slotted it past them.

In that tableau, as Trent's corner was flying toward Origi, there was a moment of disbelieving silence at Anfield, and then an explosion of noise that grew through Origi's celebration. The goal was going to count. The directors' box, typically a place of dignity and decorum, was rapidly becoming unhinged. I'd never heard it so loud in there, and had never heard it so loud inside the stadium. I glanced over to the Barca side of the directors' box to see a sea of drawn faces and heads in hands. Down on the pitch Lionel

Messi had the expression of a man who'd just arrived at an intersection that was nowhere to be found on his GPS.

Of course, there was still 11 minutes plus stoppage time to be played. I leaned over to Debbie in the din and said, "Get ready; there is going to be an onslaught, because now they're going to come after us."

But I'd overestimated Barca. They were, by this point, broken. There were some thrusts, but no chances nearly as good as what they'd had in the first half. Joe Gomez came on for the heroic Origi. Daniel Sturridge came on for Shaqiri, who'd had maybe the game of his life. In between, there was another moment of deep concern when Virgil van Dijk went down after a clash of heads and needed treatment. At this point, what was left of our bench was the backup keeper Simon Mignolet, the central defender Dejan Lovren, and two 19-year-olds, Rhian Brewster and Ben Woodburn. We got to stoppage time, and soon the crowd was singing, as per the custom:

When you walk through a storm, hold your head up high...

And then James Milner—an aging veteran whose career was revived under Klopp—took the ball to the corner, and held off two defenders, and then in the midst of the singing and all the rest, we heard the sharp whistle of the referee and the unthinkable victory was consecrated.

I celebrated and accepted hugs. Bartomeu came over and embraced me, and with grace and magnanimity, whispered in my ear, "Now go and win it."

I looked out over the pitch, where Jürgen was hugging everyone in sight. I had been coming to Anfield for sixty years by then, but I'd never experienced a night like this before. There was Salah on the field, his "Never Give Up" shirt visible to all. He and Virgil flanked the gaffer, on what became the rarest of all nights, as the whole team lined up down by the Kop and sang "You'll Never Walk Alone" for a third time.

After I cheered the lads as they came off—I always remained in the directors' box until the players themselves departed the pitch—I later saw two of the legends of my youth, Kenny Dalglish and Ian Rush. They were wearing the same expression of amazement as every other Liverpool supporter.

I looked at them and asked, "Greatest night ever at Anfield?"

They both responded in the affirmative. Nobody wanted to go home. The boardroom bar service usually shut down shortly after the game, but it stayed open late that night. My friends Andy Cooke, the head of the constabulary, and metro mayor Steve Rotheram both remained to imbibe and celebrate the magnificent achievement.

As Debbie and I finally left Anfield around midnight, I thought of the long, circuitous quest that had taken me from Merseyside to Wales and then to various spots across the United States and back again. Football had sent me on this journey, and football had brought me back home. When I finally got home, at 1 a.m., I poured myself a glass of wine and sat in the living room to watch the telecast of the game I'd just witnessed in person. It was bizarre, but I felt like I had to see it on TV to know that it had actually happened.

◆

The next morning, we started planning for the final in Madrid. On the one hand, it was an abrupt shock—nobody had been calling about provisional ticket and hotel arrangements when we trailed 3–0 in the tie, but now the whole world wanted to go to the final. It was an onslaught, but we had a club secretary, the redoubtable Danny Stanway, who had perfected the daunting task of fielding ticket requests from all corners, as well as managing communications on logistics with UEFA and the opposing club, and additionally our staff had the experience of the Kyiv final a year earlier. It's one thing to see a club handle a deluge of requests in a prompt and orderly fashion; it's another thing to witness it from the inside, to see and understand the accomplished work by the Liverpool FC staff—literally hundreds of unsung heroes who allow the club and its supporters to migrate to another country for a weekend.

The challenge—for Liverpool, and UEFA, and the city of Madrid—was that our fanbase was so broad and enthusiastic, and Madrid was so relatively close, that we had estimates of somewhere between 30,000 to 40,000 Liverpool fans *without tickets* descending on the city, above and beyond the many thousands who had procured tickets.

But before that, we had a title race to settle. It was one of the great battles in Premier League history, of two teams winning games at an unprecedented rate. Liverpool lost one match all season, the early January battle against City, and closed with a kick, winning our last nine matches—often in dramatic fashion. In consecutive matches in late March, we needed a late Milner penalty to vanquish Fulham, then a Spurs own-goal in the 90th minute to prevail in that contest. In the league season's penultimate game, another late Origi goal earned us a hard-fought 3–2 win over Newcastle. Two days later, we sat down to watch City, who had won 12 straight, but were facing a tough test against Leicester. They were being held to a cagy nil-nil draw into the 70th minute, when Vincent Kompany—captain, talisman, but about the last guy you would suspect to deliver a wonder goal—released a thunderbolt from outside the box to secure a hard-fought 1–0 win. City finished on 98 points; Liverpool on 97. The 11.7 millimeters that separated Mane's shot from completely crossing the line against City was the slender difference.

But no one was sulking. The future was bright, and Liverpool had made it back to the Champions League final, while City would have to sit and watch at home. Instead, it was Tottenham Hotspur, unlikely late winners over Ajax in the other semifinal, that we'd be meeting in Madrid.

The fan park experience in Spain was every bit as raucous and joyous as it had been the year before, and by now the singer Jamie Webster had become inextricably linked to the larger Liverpool "Boss Nights" experience. The crowd sang along to Kop odes to Virgil van Dijk, and Salah, and Trent, and, most memorably, Roberto Firmino. The streets of Madrid rang out with choruses of *Si, Señor.* There were Spurs fans in the city, but they were outnumbered greatly—5 to 1? 10 to 1? Pick a number.

On the day of the match, our club executives left ahead of the team itself, into the byzantine maze of central Madrid. And because it was the biggest single-day sporting event in the world, of course our officially sanctioned UEFA driver took the wrong exit, arriving onto a surface street that dropped us right in the midst of a traffic jam for the ages.

Fortunately, the team bus took the correct exit and got to the stadium in plenty of time. But as the traffic around the stadium built up, we were stranded in the gridlock, about a mile away from the stadium. We could see it from where we were, but the bus was not moving. At one point, John Henry made the executive decision that we were all thinking about—let's just walk it. Debbie looked great as always, though in her four-inch Christian Louboutin heels she wasn't dressed to walk a mile over rough terrain. It was a ragtag bunch that marched towards the Wanda Metropolitano. Gary McAllister had just had hip replacement surgery ten days before, Kenny Dalglish graciously offered Debbie his dress shoes so that she could slip out of her heels, while the cadre of FSG partners from Boston wondered whether this is how you always get to a Champions League final.

We finally got to the stadium in time for kickoff. It was a curious feeling. A year earlier, against Real Madrid in Kyiv, we'd just been happy to be there. Now, having lost the league by a single point and having miraculously rallied past Barca in the semifinal, we felt like we *had* to win. We were also dealing with the prospect of Jürgen's record in tournament finals. We'd lost both a League Cup final and a Europa League final in 2016 and the Champions League final in 2018, and he'd lost his last three finals with Dortmund. The press was quick to remind everyone that our gaffer had lost six finals in a row.

Yet even before kickoff, I and most everyone around me felt calmly confident. We knew we were better than Spurs—we'd already beaten them twice in the league—and felt sure we would prove that. Mo Salah's penalty conversion in the second minute was the ideal way to start the match. And Origi's goal on 87 minutes was the clincher, starting a celebration that had been a year in the making, and splendidly confirming Jürgen's boozy claim from Kyiv.

The ensuing team party back at the hotel was nearly an all-night affair, with Big Ears making the rounds and a feeling of profound togetherness and satisfaction everywhere. I was surrounded by friends and family, and a sublime feeling of accomplishment. What I remember best about the party was Xherdan Shaqiri chatting up my daughter Toni-Marie, who did a marvelous job handling herself. Tara and Tyler were there as well, all drinking in this unforgettable moment in our lives. In the midst of the celebration, you sensed the larger resonance: It wasn't just the club and staff partying in Madrid. We knew that Merseyside was rocking through the night, and other jubilant cohorts of Liverpool fans were celebrating literally all over the world. I lasted until around 4:30 in the morning, when I realized I needed to get up to our room, take a quick shower and start packing for our 7 a.m. flight back to Liverpool John Lennon Airport.

When we arrived back on Merseyside, we had only a couple of hours to recharge before reporting to Melwood, and then on to Allerton to start the open-top bus parade. In yet another circle of life moment, we jumped on the buses only 200 yards from Springwood Heath Primary School, which I had attended when we lived above the Gay Cavalier pub fifty-six years before. By now, I'd spent the previous two years living in the city and representing Liverpool around the world. I knew about as well as anyone how deep the loyalty to the club ran. But even I wasn't quite prepared for the scale or the degree of adulation that greeted our convoy, the reported 700,000 who turned out on the streets of the city, an amazing number when you consider that we had left 50–60,000 of our most devout fans back in Madrid, unable to get flights back to Liverpool until later in the day

On the parade route, I was on the bus with Virgil and Robbo and Hendo and Jürgen. I felt somewhat out of place, but John Henry was on that bus and asked me to join him. Players were taking turns lifting Big Ears, but I steered clear—I was glad the club had won it, though well aware that I had no business touching that iconic trophy.

But at one point, I pulled up a picture on my phone of my dad during his Red Lion days, and I asked my amazing executive assistant, Tina Roberts, to take a picture of me holding the photograph up during the parade. The journey had been long, but I was back home, and he was on the bus with me. I'd come full circle. You really can go home again.

The next offseason would see Liverpool continuing the virtuous cycle, all the while focusing on the one prize that had eluded us: the Premier League championship. It had been thirty years since the Reds had topped the domestic league, and in that time—Alex Ferguson's Man United having famously knocked us off our perch—we'd been usurped as the winner of the most league titles. That was the one prize that had eluded Liverpool under Jürgen Klopp, and everyone involved seemed focused on ending the thirty-year wait for a league title.

We would all come back in August, on a mission.

CHAPTER FIFTEEN

THE BEST OF TIMES, THE WORST OF TIMES

So much of sports is about anticipation. The coming season, the coming challenge, the big game circled on the calendar. Going into the 2019/20 campaign, there were lots of circles on the calendar. It promised to be the busiest season in the history of Liverpool Football Club. We wouldn't merely be competing on four fronts—the Premier League, the FA Cup, the League Cup, and the Champions League—but we'd also be 1) playing three matches in six days on a pre-season tour of America in late July, 2) facing Manchester City at Wembley in the Community Shield in early August, 3) playing Chelsea 11 days later—five days after the league opener—in the UEFA Super Cup in Istanbul, and 4) traveling to Qatar in the middle of the already crowded festive season to compete in the FIFA Club World Cup.

All the matches were important, but it was clear in everyone's mind that the first priority was the league, which Liverpool hadn't won since 1990, back when it was the First Division, and which had been so tantalizingly close the previous spring.

There weren't a lot of high-profile additions to the team that summer. We signed the young Fulham phenomenon Harvey Elliott, but he didn't figure to find much playing time during the season. Our squad was maturing, experienced, and ready to mount another title challenge.

From my standpoint, things on the business side were going well. Plans had begun in earnest on the long-awaited

Anfield Road end expansion, and the development of a state-of-the-art training facility at Kirkby, the demands of top-flight football having exceeded the space and capabilities of Melwood. We were moving decisively into the mobile and digital realms, working with head of ticketing Phil Dutton on the first season of all-digital ticketing. I was spending a good portion of my office time working on Project Fan Connect with our marketing and IT teams, as we strove to improve our online presence and efficiency. On my trips to Asia, we found several partners interested in opening dedicated Liverpool FC concept stores, in recognition of the club's broad support on the continent. Meanwhile, we continued our efforts to increase fan engagement in the digital realm, with the growing popularity of the marvelous *Inside Anfield* video series produced by our in-house team at LFC.tv. As fans, peering in from the outside, we take much of this for granted, but I can tell you that this incessant grind to improve, innovate, and engage inside a global football club, as I saw it and lived it from within, is impressive and matched anything I had experienced in previous careers in Silicon Valley. Unseen and unsung heroes all...

I was also in discussions with Billy Hogan about what to do about the team's kit contract. The design team at New Balance had consistently done a marvelous job, and every new iteration of the Liverpool kit felt bespoke and imaginative. A few of the most compelling designs—like the classic long-sleeve goalkeeper's jersey in 2019/20—seemed to be on backorder for much of the season. And therein was the problem: New Balance had the design capabilities to handle the Liverpool account, but the company lacked the worldwide distribution that the club by now needed. New Balance simply couldn't manufacture the kits and other material fast enough to keep their retail distributors—or our online pro shop—in stock. It was frustrating for us, and for our supporters, and it violated one of the simplest tenets of business: When people are trying to give you their money, you shouldn't make them wait.

In the coming months, Billy negotiated a deal with Nike (to start with the 2020/21 season), which offered a much more vigorous distribution channel. It was an innovative agreement, with Nike paying less up front but offering a greater percentage return after sales met a certain threshold, which we were certain they would do. The messy end of the process wound up with New Balance suing to keep the contract, but the court saw it the way we did—Nike offered broader global exposure that New Balance simply couldn't match, and also lacked the prestige of Nike's not-so-secret weapon, LFC co-owner (with a small stake) LeBron James.

We lost the Community Shield to City on penalties, then won the UEFA Super Cup against Chelsea on penalties, with the veteran keeper Adrian—signed to replace Simon Mignolet after he returned home to Belgium to play for Club Brugge—making the match-winning save in the shootout. By then it was clear that the front line of Salah, Mane, and Firmino had retained this otherworldly sense of near-telepathic communication. They were so much fun to watch, thrilling in their interplay but never purely for show. Even Firmino's flourishes—like his patented no-look goals—carried a zest for the game without ever disrespecting it.

We started off winning and just kept our foot on the gas. Scored 15 goals in our first five league matches, all wins. The fifth was a 12:30 kickoff against Newcastle, which saw the Geordies go ahead early and then the Reds storm back for a 3–1 win. Later that Saturday, Manchester City—who had already dropped points in an early 2–2 draw with Spurs—went to Carrow Road to play recently promoted Norwich City, and their remarkable Finnish striker Teemu Pukki. His 50th-minute goal put Norwich up 3–1, and they held on for an utterly improbable 3–2 win.

Like all of the Liverpool supporters, I was giddy. In the thrall of the moment, I couldn't resist posting a tweet consisting of nothing but a canary emoji. As I sat there looking at my phone, the tweet racked up something like 3,000 likes in the first two minutes it was posted. At which point I came to my senses, realizing immediately how unprofessional this was. I had just deleted the tweet when I received a message on WhatsApp from HQ in Boston.

"I see you tweeted a canary. Take it down."

"Yes, stupid of me," I replied. "I've already deleted it. Sorry."

Suitably chastened, I tweeted more carefully thereafter.

◆

In the summer of 2019, Liverpool FC had applied to trademark the Liverpool name in a football context. The impetus was all the counterfeit goods coming from large Asian retailers, particularly the ubiquitous e-commerce sites dealing in dodgy merchandise. Many other clubs—Tottenham, Everton, and Chelsea among them—had done the same. When counterfeit 50/50 scarves for the Liverpool–Spurs Champions League final hit the streets of Madrid, we couldn't do anything, but instead had to rely on the lawyers at Tottenham to shut it down.

Our reasons were sound, but inevitably the news of the application—Liverpool FC trying to trademark the name Liverpool—aroused the suspicion of the Spirit of Shankly supporters' group, the smaller football clubs in the area—like South Liverpool FC—and many of the independent creatives like Ian Maloney at Love Follow Conquer, Jocky at Transalpino, and Mick and Michelle Deane at Hat Scarf or a Badge. There was an entire subculture of these designers, ranging from tiny shops to more established outlets like the Anfield Wrap, that made great merchandise and were almost always careful to steer clear of any obvious existing trademark violations. They were a key part of the unique supporters' culture that we embraced and encouraged.

Wanting to address their understandable concerns, I called a meeting at Chapel Street to make clear that we weren't going after the independents—I had a few of their shirts myself—but rather trying to protect the club from the counterfeiters who were flooding the market. The dialogue was valuable. I'll concede that some of those in SOS and among the independent creatives remained unconvinced, but they at least came to understand why we felt it necessary to apply for the trademark. We, in turn, recognized the local independent manufacturers who were concerned that even if we didn't overstep our bounds now, a trademark could present problems at some time in the future, if and when FSG sold its majority interest. We both had credible reasons, LFC for concern about counterfeiting, and the independent creatives for concern about corporate overreach. Ultimately, the Intellectual Property Office said we couldn't get the trademark, because "the geographical significance" of the place was greater than in the case of other Premier League clubs. We accepted the decision, but the dialogue was part of a greater sense of transparency and communication between the club and its supporters.

Meanwhile, the season was hurtling forward and only a 1–1 draw at Old Trafford had marred our otherwise perfect league record. Even when Klopp was putting out a younger side—as in the fourth round of the League Cup at home against Arsenal in late October—there was this sense of self-belief coursing through the team, no matter who was out there. Klopp made 11 changes from our win over Spurs three days earlier, and the mostly young squad—including 18-year-old Liverpool native Curtis Jones, making his Anfield debut—trailed 3–1, 4–2, and 5–4 in stoppage time before Divock Origi (it's that man again) equalized at 90+4 minutes. Caoimhin Kelleher made the penalty shootout save and we emerged from a game that made no sense whatsoever, with the teenager Jones striking the winning penalty to win it in front of an ecstatic and astonished Kop.

Good vibes aside, we knew the real showdown would come November 10. It was a crucial home fixture against Manchester City. It was also a special day for me. The organizers of the Liverpool TEDx conference had invited me to give a TED talk that day. So as we waited for the 4:30 kickoff between Liverpool and Man City, I spent the morning at the Echo Arena, speaking about my career and my secret weapon—having been born in Liverpool—in a 16-minute talk titled "The Power of Scouseness."

After the TED talk, I changed into my suit in the bathroom of the arena and headed to Anfield for the battle. These games were almost always taut and nervy, but also bracing, because the Liverpool–Man City matches in the Klopp/Guardiola era were played at such a rarefied level. Going into the match with a six-point lead at the top of the table, it was clear what was at stake: A Man City win would put them within striking distance, only three points off the pace. A Liverpool win would put us up by nine points, and deliver the message that this season was different.

We had that incredible front line, that sturdy engine room of a midfield, that back line anchored by the world's best center back, Virgil van Dijk, and arguably the world's best keeper in Alisson. In Jürgen Klopp we also had the only manager who had a winning record against Pep Guardiola. All of it came together that day. Fabinho's worldie thunderbolt from distance put Liverpool up early, then a magnificent delivery from Andy Robertson that Salah headed in put us up 2–0. Mane's header past Claudio Bravo's near post made it 3–0, and though City pegged one back, it was still a comprehensive 3–1 win. Still the Kop didn't sing about winning the league. The mindset, from the players to the supporters was clear: One game at a time.

The next obstacle came in December, an always complicated and crowded schedule, which was further complicated by Liverpool needing to play two games on another continent—Qatar for the FIFA Club World Cup—a week before Christmas. One of the things that Jürgen had spoken about repeatedly in his time at Liverpool was the ludicrously crowded fixture schedule, especially for Premier League teams. It went from bad to worse during the festive season and was further exacerbated by the anachronistic FA Cup replays, and the bloated two-legged semifinal ties in the League Cup. It was all too much, and he made this point frequently, not only when Liverpool were being hurt by these scheduling inanities.

The issue came to a boil in December, when Liverpool's first match in the FIFA Club World Cup (December 18) happened just a day after the Fourth Round tie in the FA Cup (December 17). Klopp and the senior squad were already getting their bearings in Doha when the junior team faced Villa in the FA Cup.

Some had been calling for Jürgen to send the juniors to Qatar and focus on the domestic campaign. But that's not how he—or we—were wired. Liverpool had never won the Club World Cup, and so this was another major trophy that we were fighting for. It took a tough opening win over Monterrey (aided by a late Firmino goal) to get to the final, where we wound up in extra time against Flamengo of Brazil (needing and getting yet another late Firmino goal) before winning it.

The team returned to England, jet-lagged and on short rest, knowing we had to face Leicester on Boxing Day. Brendan Rodgers's side was formidable and dangerous, and trailing us by only eight points. That was the day I truly marveled at the resilience of this team.

We held a 1–0 lead until the 71st minute, when we were awarded a penalty on a handball in the box. James Milner stepped up to the spot, and as he was doing so, I leaned over to Debbie and said, "If he makes this, we're going to win the league." I had been physically present at every game that season thus far, and I knew that this was our biggest challenge to date. Leicester had been pressing hard for an equalizer, but you could sense if we went two up their heads would drop. Millie converted, thumping it down the middle, and we added two goals later for a comprehensive 4–0 thrashing, which put the rest of the league on notice that this side wasn't going to be easy to catch. Even in the away end, in the jubilation of that moment, the visiting supporters didn't sing about winning the league.

Nearly a month later, the day finally arrived. Liverpool at home against Manchester United. At that point—matchday 22—United were the only side to have taken points off Liverpool. That, combined with the always ferocious rivalry, made it a fraught, pressurized day. Virgil's early header put the Reds up, but a couple of other goals were disallowed and as we went into stoppage time the score remained 1–0. United got a corner and everyone held their breath, but after Alisson collected and spotted Mo Salah running free, he found him with a remarkably targeted side volley, and Salah fought off two defenders, slotting past David de Gea to kill the game. Then he tore off his jersey—exposing the world to his sculpted six-pack abs—and prompted the Kop, at long last, to sing:

We're gonna win the league, We're gonna win the league,
Now you gonna believe us, Now you gonna believe us,
Now you gonna believe us, We're gonna win the league...

It was a magnificent feeling. A week and a half later, January 30, we held a ceremony to unveil the Bob Paisley statue outside of Anfield. Kenny Dalglish—Paisley's very first signing—pulled the sheet at the unveiling, and Paisley's other former players came by the dozens. The project had been the brainchild of my friend, the sculptor Emma Rodgers, who one day in 2018, after me showing her the iconic picture of the then-assistant coach Paisley carrying the injured Red stalwart Emlyn Hughes off the pitch, asked if she could borrow it for a while. A few months later, Emma asked me to stop by the Castle Fine Arts Foundry in the Baltic Triangle, where she often worked. When I walked in, she showed me a maquette of the picture brought to life in a sculpture by the accomplished artist Andy Edwards, who'd created the Beatles statues at the waterfront in Liverpool, and the majestic Christmas truce statue in front of the bombed-out St. Luke's Church, depicting British and German troops playing a game of football on Christmas Day during World War I.

As soon as I saw the maquette, I knew instantly that a full-sized sculpture would be an iconic addition to the space around Anfield. I talked with Edwards about his vision ("I'm a Derby County fan," he explained, "but I've always admired what Paisley meant to the club, and always thought he deserved a statue"). Chris Butler, the owner of the foundry and a dedicated Liverpool fan, took me in some detail through what it would take to get from maquette to an 8-foot tall bronze statue.

The great Shankly statue had been funded by the Carlsberg beer people, our shirt sponsor for the better part of twenty years. In that spirit, I contacted the executives at Standard Chartered, the club's shirt sponsor since 2010, and pitched them on the value of adding their own permanent addition to Liverpool's gameday experience. Caroline Darcy, the head of Standard Chartered's global sponsorship group, agreed to fund the six-figure project, and I'll never forget the look of pride in the eyes of Paisley's children, and the way Edwards's marvelously rendered sculpture brought the photograph to life, embodying everything about what the club stood for. The modern LFC was built on the shoulders of giants, something that should be remembered and celebrated, and those individuals whose blood, sweat, and tears built this club should be always revered.

It was a thrilling time. Liverpool FC were rampant on the field, and the business side was also performing remarkably well, reaching out to fans, doing good work in the community, selling shirts as fast as they could be manufactured, acting as a flywheel to the virtuous cycle. I was ecstatic as a fan, and also so proud of everything we'd accomplished. The collective work of the tireless "team behind the team" at Liverpool FC was acknowledged when I received the Premier League CEO of the Year award in November 2019, recognizing the amazing progress we had made off the pitch in support of Jürgen's relentless quest for trophies. Everything seemed to be coming together well in every facet of the club.

Yet I was also harboring a heartbreaking secret I knew I'd need to keep through the end of the season.

◆

When I was offered the job back in the fall of 2016, I knew it involved a considerable career risk. For starters, I was leaving a lot of money on the table—I stood to receive several million dollars in vested equity if I'd merely stayed at EA. I was also taking a compensation cut to move from EA to Liverpool FC, but that really wasn't important to me at this point in my career. Given the leap of faith I was making, I'd asked for a four-year contract. But FSG executives were adamant that all they could offer was three years. And that was fine. I was an unknown quantity and needed to prove myself. I was confident I could do the job well.

And I believe I did. The real problem, it seemed, was that my social media presence was deemed "unstatesmanlike," a term that came up more than once.

"You're known as Peter the tweeter," I was told.

The term, however clever, seemed high-schoolish to me, but I was willing to live with it. I understood that other executives wanted to keep a low profile. I understood that I was perhaps the only CEO in the Premier League with an active social media presence. But I restated the point: I wasn't doing it to feed my ego, or because I was starved for attention. I was doing it because I was convinced that this world-class football club with an absentee ownership group needed to connect with its supporters. Jürgen and head of communications Susan Black did this marvelously on the football side. But no one had done it on the business side and taken advantage of the platforms now available to communicate directly and in real time with our supporters.

By the summer of 2019, as our successes mounted, I was keenly aware that my contract renewal hadn't been discussed. I finally pressed Mike Gordon on the point, and he agreed we'd talk about it when he was next in Liverpool, in October. He came into my office on Chapel Street late one afternoon, after most of the staff had left. He closed the door, sat down, and his opening words were, "I think we're going to do something different." He didn't really elaborate on that, simply informing me that FSG had decided not to renew my contract. I was stunned but left with the agreement that neither side would reveal the news until the end of the 2019/20 season.

The English talk about the stiff upper lip. I wasn't going to detract from potentially the greatest season in Liverpool history. I was well aware this wasn't about me. I worked for the club because I loved the club, and thought my skills and business experience could make a difference. So I determined that I was going to do two things: 1) Continue performing to the absolute best of my abilities during the time I had remaining as Liverpool CEO, and 2) Savor and appreciate every minute of our dream season that we had left. Subsequent events would make both of those goals extremely challenging.

◆

We heard the word coronavirus for the first time in January. Around the house, Debbie and I regularly had the TV tuned to CNN International. That month, we began to hear about the mysterious virus, and then the isolated reports of it breaking out of China. Even after Wuhan was placed under lockdown in late January, there was still some casual flippancy about it in the West. "Just a nasty strain of the 'flu." News grew worse in February, and the response from the White House at the time seemed willfully misguided—the mindset seemed to be to do nothing that might threaten the economy. But of course, Covid would threaten the economy everywhere.

In early March, before the second leg of the Champions League quarterfinal against Atletico Madrid, I got a call from the Premier League CEO Richard Masters.

"Hey, look, here's the deal," he said. "We're getting more than a little worried here. You're playing at Goodison Park next weekend. And if you beat Everton, you've got Palace at Anfield. If you win that game as well, then you'll have won the League. Would you be willing—because we're very worried about this virus—would you be willing to accept the Premier League trophy that day at home against Palace?"

I said, "Of course," but I also grasped by the urgency in Richard's voice that we were facing something unprecedented.

The rest of that week was surreal. Madrid, after shutting down all activities in the city, still allowed 3,000 Atletico supporters to come to the UK. They walked and talked and drank all around Liverpool. We'd already had grave doubts about the game and the possible transmission of the virus, but UEFA was adamant: either we play the game, or we forfeit. The second leg of that quarterfinal was scintillating, with Roberto Firmino's extra-time goal leaving Liverpool poised to go through. But credit to Diego Simeone and his squad, they fought back and prevailed.

The rest of the week was a microcosm of the uncertainty. One day, the Premier League announced defiantly it would go ahead with its games. In a matter of hours, Arsenal manager Mikel Arteta tested positive for Covid, and the ludicrousness of going ahead with the games became obvious. The next day, the Premier League shut everything down.

That began the weirdest period in my professional career or, for that matter, my entire life. Suddenly, and quite sensibly, everything got shut down, people started rinsing all their vegetables, wiping down the cardboard boxes of their home deliveries, and washing their hands for an entire rendition of Happy Birthday. In the UK, you could only be outside for 90 minutes a day on a walk, and strict social-distancing protocols were implemented everywhere.

Meanwhile, I was attending regular conference calls via Microsoft Teams during which the Premier League was deciding how to proceed, and separate informal calls with executives from other clubs. What came out of those Premier League meetings, at a time when every club in the league was still paying its players and all of its staff, was that, to the extent possible, we *had* to find a way to finish the season, and in the process secure the payment from our broadcast partners, thus avoiding what could have been a financial Armageddon.

Then it became a more practical question: How do we play games behind closed doors? How do we keep players safe? How do we keep the training staff safe?

It was a little bit surprising (or maybe not) how eager the teams in danger of relegation—especially those already hovering at the bottom of the table—were to declare the entire season "null and void." Those clearly self-interested ploys were quickly dismissed, although not without some terse back and forth and raised voices. Eventually cooler heads prevailed. There was the entire area of the integrity of the sport to consider, and the significant fact that we were 25 points clear and on the verge of winning the league *already.*

It was during this time that the British government

offered a furlough scheme to companies. As a tax-paying entity, LFC was eligible, and since we were still paying staff and players—while bringing in virtually no revenue—we agreed to take advantage of it. When Liverpool announced it was accepting the furlough plan, there was an outcry in the city. It reminded me again, as if I needed it, that Liverpool really was exceptional. Other teams had done the same without anywhere near the blowback. After long discussions, we agreed to pull out of the plan and find a way to continue paying our staff. I issued a public letter of apology, stating that we had come to the "wrong conclusion" in our decision to apply for the government's Coronavirus Job Retention Scheme, and that we would continue to support our staff financially solely from the club's own resources. Taking care of our people at this most difficult of times was paramount and we admitted the error of our ways and moved on.

In the meantime, the league pushed toward Project Restart. Finally on June 21—more than three months after our last match—Liverpool took the field against Everton behind closed doors at Goodison Park. I'll never forget the surreal scene. In the empty stadium, you could hear the booming baritone of Virgil van Dijk commanding the back line ("Second ball!"), as well as the constant filibuster of team captain Jordan Henderson, calling for the ball, commanding and scolding his teammates in turn. Meanwhile, through all of it, there was a bloke across the street from Goodison who spent much of the game practicing on his trumpet, his strained notes clearly audible above the fray.

After beating Crystal Palace in the first home game since the restart, Liverpool were on the verge of mathematically clinching it. Jürgen wisely informed the team that whenever it might happen, they needed to be together. So they gathered at Formby Hall for the Man City–Chelsea match, no one expecting much more than an easy City win. But when

Chelsea prevailed, the celebration began, among the team, then emanating around the world.

Debbie and I were at home. I'd been carrying around a bottle of Liverpool FC-branded champagne for the better part of twenty years. I'd vowed to open it when Liverpool finally won the league again. I put it on ice near the end of the match, then popped the cork with Debbie after it went final. The wine was pretty much vinegar by that point, but we celebrated nonetheless, including a toast to the heavens for my dad.

The rest of the season was a blur. Many supporters—and perhaps a player or two—were still hung over from partying when we faced Manchester City a week later. What I remember best about that game is Bernardo Silva peeling off the guard of honor even before our last player, Mo Salah, could walk through it. Man City's 4–0 win was an annoyance, but it couldn't stop the party.

For the last home game—versus Chelsea—we'd made plans to lift the Premier League trophy on the Kop—which would be empty, but still, it was the right place. Even that day of joy turned into a stressful cliffhanger. The morning of the match, we couldn't get the routine safety certificate signed to go ahead with the match, as we had applied for permission for the players and coaching staff's families to attend the game and join in the festivities in the evening. I spent the day making calls all over the country—to the Premier League offices, to 10 Downing Street, to the Liverpool Mayor's office. Finally it was up to the Liverpool City Council CEO Tony Reeves, whom I'd interrupted on holiday, to drive back to the city and get it all sorted. Late that afternoon, we finally got the certificate signed, allowing the families of the players and coaches to sit—out of the TV cameras' view—in Box 1A, then celebrate with them after the match.

I watched the scene, with the players coming up one by one to get their medals, and I thought again how thrilled my dad would have been to see it all. In front of the Kop, I shared a champagne toast with Ian Rush and Kenny Dalglish, and we celebrated LFC being back on our perch. Where we belonged.

◆

The season concluded on July 26 and five days later, on July 31, 2020, we made the announcement that I was leaving as Liverpool's CEO. That was my last day in the office. The contract was up, and now it was time to go back to California. I took out a full-page ad in the *Echo*, thanking the club, the staff, the gaffer, the players, and the city for welcoming me home.

I was bruised. A number of local journalists, understandably, dug deeper into the story and reported that my contract was not being renewed. While I understood they were doing their job, it didn't make the stories any less painful. I couldn't even bear to tell my own children the full story. I just said I was looking forward to being closer to them, and that Debbie was looking forward to returning to California weather, both of which were true. We knew we had to sell Axholme. I was out of a job—I'd only come back to England for that one job—and now it was time to return to America.

In the end, I was still convinced I did the right thing. Leading from the front, being verbal, leaning in to representing the club, both to our colleagues in the Premier League and Europe, and our supporters around the world. Given that the owners were another continent away, I thought it was important to reach out to our supporters and our fellow competitors, to let them know we understood our history and our support, and try to put a human face on the business side. I left feeling proud of what we'd accomplished. To this day, when I return to Liverpool and walk the streets, people will stop me and say hello and shake my hand, The usual salutation is not about winning trophies during my time there, or the club being in a better financial situation. It's some variation on, "You made me feel closer to the club." Isn't that what all fans want? If that's my legacy, then that's good enough for me.

As it turned out, what FSG ultimately wanted was maybe a different type of CEO, and I'm self-aware enough to recognize I pushed some boundaries that in retrospect I should have stayed away from. Believe me, I got to meet a myriad of Premier League owners, and it is clear to me to this day that FSG stand head and shoulders above just about anyone else. I supported the great majority of their decisions, and they may have been right about this as well. This was something about which reasonable people could differ.

The question comes up: If I knew then what I know now, would I have still taken the job again?

In a second, yes, without a moment's hesitation.

It was the job of a lifetime, even if it only lasted for three and a half years.

CHAPTER SIXTEEN

COME TOGETHER

As I prepared to leave Liverpool, I was faced with a daunting existential question: What do you do after you've finished the dream job of a lifetime?

You don't stop living, for one thing. And you don't stop dreaming, for another.

Debbie and I returned to California, and found a home in Montecito, a suburb of Santa Barbara. There we settled down with her ailing mom, and her Great Dane Diego, and tried to figure out what was next. It wasn't so much a question of needing to find work—although in California, literally everything is more expensive—as much as wanting to continue doing something meaningful.

In those first few months, I discovered something. Though I had stepped away from the Beautiful Game, the sport kept calling me back, from one direction or another.

◆

Even before I'd returned to the States, I received a call from my friend Steve Horowitz at Inner Circle Sports, which specializes in finding buyers and sellers for professional sports teams. Steve said he was representing some investors looking to buy a depressed British soccer team at the bottom of the pyramid, and make a documentary about the journey.

You probably know the rest: One of the investors turned out to be Rob McElhenney, the actor and producer from *It's Always Sunny in Philadelphia* and *Mythic Quest*, a hardcore sports fan, who was—along with the actor Ryan Reynolds—zeroing in on making the purchase. After considering a range of options, they focused on Wrexham AFC, the club I had grown up watching when living in Marford, and which played its games at the Racecourse Ground, the oldest international football stadium in the world still in use today (and the same stadium in which I had played some of my biggest junior matches).

In February 2021, I was in Montecito, and Rob drove up from LA, wanting to pick my brain because he and Ryan very much didn't want to seem to be two callow, privileged actors who were buying a club on a lark. They both understood that the relationship between a club and its community ran deep.

I talked Rob through the history of Wrexham and about the challenges faced by both the club and the community. I told him that if he and Ryan were truly committed to being stewards of Wrexham AFC, and ushering them back into the Football League, they would be heroes in the town. Rob was committed, and so enthusiastic that he staged a full-court charm offensive in trying to convince me to return to the UK and become Wrexham's new CEO.

"Sorry, mate," I said. "It's not going to happen. I appreciate the offer, but there is no way I'm going from the CEO of Liverpool FC and then return to California, only to turn right back around and become the CEO of Wrexham AFC. I'll be glad to be a resource and an official advisor, because I have deep and lengthy relationship with the club, and I will help you in any way I can, but my home is here now."

I spent the next couple of months doing interviews with the likes of the BBC and Bloomberg, as I saw one of the key elements of my role as an advisor was convincing all of the stakeholders that Rob and Ryan were committed long-term to the club, with the goal of restoring it to the Football League and simultaneously bringing pride back to a community that had seen so much societal and economic upheaval in the decades previous.

Later, with a small sense of pride, I watched, along with the rest of the world, as the documentary captured the imagination of football fans (and many non-football fans) all around the world. I heard glowing reports from my brother Andy, who was a longtime Wrexham fan and knew many of the key locals. Before the first season aired, I helped out Rob and Ryan by calling on my old friends at EA Sports, and helping to arrange getting Wrexham included as one of the clubs in the *FIFA* game.

And back in Wrexham, a town that had fallen on hard times and whose football club had gone into administration, there was a remarkable rebirth, a sporting and civic renaissance still playing out today, shared with a global audience that cheer for the likes of Paul Mullin and Ollie Palmer and seemingly know everything about little old Wrexham. Still amusingly bizarre to me.

◆

Though I had left Liverpool, the club never left me. Instead of watching the matches in the directors' box at Anfield or rival stadiums, I now watched them in my living room on mornings in Montecito. Debbie's mom, Amelia "Molly" Mills, had moved in with us, and I soon converted this wonderful, feisty, stubborn, generous Mexican immigrant from her Club America football club to Liverpool FC. Molly and I watched innumerable games together. She was a trooper, even getting up for those early kickoffs that started at 4:30 a.m. in California. She came to especially love "the curly one," Mohamed Salah.

For the more reasonable kickoff times, I eventually found my way to Dargan's, a proper Irish pub in downtown Santa

Barbara, where that city's chapter of the Official Liverpool Supporters Club met for all the matches. I obviously missed my old gig, but it was good to be able to fully emote again, and call the ref a wanker when it was warranted, which was maddeningly often.

The football world was rocked—and I was saddened—in April 2021 when the European Super League was announced, with Liverpool one of the 12 clubs vowing to join the breakaway enterprise. I had heard some vague rumblings when I was CEO, but nothing that would indicate that this would become a reality. During that week, when the Super League was presented as inevitable and, only days later, collapsed under the weight of public opposition and its own logical contradictions, I was asked more than once what I would have done if I had been the Liverpool CEO at the time. The answer is I couldn't have done much. I certainly would have tried to explain to FSG the inevitable and entirely understandable virulent opposition among fans, and the way the Super League idea struck at the heart of the entire ethos of meritocracy on which the football pyramid in England, and the rest of Europe, was built.

As it was, I was just another outraged fan. I went to Twitter and posted, "When we had nothing, we had the footie. We had St. John, Hunt and Callaghan. Shankly came and gave us our pride back, and put hope in our hearts. We lived for 3pm on Saturday. The Boys Pen, the Paddock, the unbridled, euphoric mayhem that was The Kop … Look after your car for sixpence? The sense of optimism in an otherwise hard grafting life. Affinity to the only thing that, for many, gave them self-worth. The highs and lows of winning and losing. Now, at the end of this storm … what? #YNWA."

For me, the entire debacle underlined something that can't be ignored. There's a temptation, when you're successful, to always build on that success. Football club owners come from all over the world, but in almost every single case they view themselves as builders. Given the success of an enterprise, they can't help but gauge its continued upward velocity by growing profits, and pursuing anything that promises to bring more revenue. This is particularly true in the Premier League, where there are clubs that seem to have budgets that are figurative bottomless pits.

At some point, one has to take the longer, more human view. Does $10 million more in the next fiscal year justify alienating a large portion of your fanbase, and jeopardizing the compelling domestic competitions on which international football has been built? It doesn't, and it didn't, and one of the great victories of football supporters in the twenty-first century was the universal pushback against the Super League and the accompanying breakdown. One only hopes the powers that be have learned their lesson. (On this, I am less confident.)

There was a sense of relief when the Super League idea was abandoned, and John Henry did the stand-up thing, circulating a video apologizing for the misstep, and promising that supporters would be more involved in any future decisions. John is the quintessential capitalist, but he has a soft, empathetic side to his personality that I thought shone through in that message of apology to the supporters.

The 2021/22 season brought a return of normalcy, and a return to the excellence that had become customary under Jürgen Klopp. I can't lie. There were still some hurt feelings—bruised ego and a measure of swallowed pride—from when I left Liverpool. But the club you love is the club you love, and the old urge remained to get back to Anfield whenever possible.

In late October, I returned to Liverpool and brought Debbie along for her first game watching from the Kop, and my first game on the Kop in probably thirty years. We managed to purchase terrific seats, about two-thirds of the way up, right behind the goal. Debbie's experience of games at Anfield had been as my wing woman and co-host in the boardroom. But she was game for the Kop experience. We met some family members at the Northwestern Hotel by Lime Street Station, then caught the Soccer Bus to Anfield. Once we found our seats, we happened to be seated nearby Eamon Preston, the folk-hero Liverpool supporter who is blind, but goes to all the matches, home and away. On the Kop, Eamon has for years been a hugely influential figure, listening to the game on his transistor radio and getting further insight from his mate Tage, then serving as the section's de facto song leader, starting the chants and anthems to respond to the action on the field. Debbie was as comfortable in jeans and trainers on the Kop as she was in cocktail dresses and high-heels in the boardroom. It was a marvelous time, though somewhat undercut by Brighton rallying from 2–0 down to draw.

That 21/22 season took on a charmed quality, with Liverpool fighting on four fronts, and that magnificent front line—the Fab Three of Salah, Mane, and Firmino—operating at a rarefied level. In spring of 2022, I flew back to London for both cup finals in Wembley, when Liverpool beat Chelsea twice to win the League Cup (with the wild 22-kick shootout at the end of extra time) and the FA Cup (with the nearly-as-wild 12-kick shootout).

On June 1, 2022, Debbie and I were among the lucky ones to be able to purchase tickets to the Champions League final in Paris. It felt like a proper denouement to a three-act Champions League play. A young and still slightly naïve Liverpool side had lost to Real Madrid in 2018. Then the Mentality Monsters returned the next year to defeat Spurs. There was the Covid interruption that followed the valiant second-leg loss to Atletico that ended the 2020 Champions League campaign, then the behind-closed-doors fugue state of 20/21. Now the Reds were completing the long, exhilarating, exhausting chase for the Quad—having won two cups and finished just a point shy of City again in the league. The

Champions League final, again facing Real Madrid, offered a chance to put an exclamation point on one of the greatest seasons in the history of club football.

Kickoff was 9 p.m. local time, but being veterans of big matches, we arrived more than two hours before. As we approached the stadium, in a throng of Liverpool fans heading toward one side, it soon became clear that a pedestrian bottleneck was developing. Soon enough, the cause was obvious—a series of French security vehicles were parked across the roadway, creating an obstacle that only a few people at a time could get through. The people waiting were vulnerable to a large assemblage of local petty thieves and pickpockets who were operating on the periphery.

While waiting to get to a ticket checkpoint ahead, the group clogged and soon it became clear that order was breaking down. If you were a certain age, old enough to remember Hillsborough, the inevitable eventually happened: You caught the eyes of another fan your age, and you shared a look of grave concern. After an hour, we finally inched to the top of the ramp only to see massive lines of LFC fans waiting at Gates Y and Z, even as those gates were closed.

The delay was unforgivable; UEFA had turned security over to the French police, and the French police were spoiling for a fight. I can't emphasize enough the extraordinary forbearance shown on the part of the Liverpool fans.

When we finally got in, minutes before 9 p.m., we saw on the video screens an official UEFA announcement over the PA that the kickoff time had been delayed for a half-hour, due to "the late arrival of fans." Everyone among the Liverpool supporters knew this was bullshit; I mentioned to Debbie that this was how the spiral of lies spread by the South Yorkshire Police Department started in 1989.

I had to do something, so I texted my friend Giorgio Marchetti, the gregarious and urbane UEFA executive who could each year be seen presiding over the ping-pong balls in the UEFA Champions League draw. I'd socialized with Giorgio over the years and knew him well. I texted him just moments after the announcement:

"Hi, Giorgio, it's Peter Moore. I can't tell you how bad things are outside the stadium. Every fundamental error in flow and access has been made this evening. Debbie and I were outside since 18.00 hrs. Nearly two hours later we got in. To blame the fans for 'late arrival' is disgraceful."

He didn't reply then. In fact, he never replied.

More to the point, UEFA didn't recant its comment—until forced to much later.

The match felt odd, disjointed. We finally saw the Liverpool fans walking in and they all looked like they'd been through the wringer, because of course they had.

Real won 1–0, as Thibaut Courtois had the game of his life. The narrative was that Liverpool were exhausted from their quest for four trophies. The truth was something both more basic and more subtle. There was a sense of unease in the crowd, and it was felt throughout the stadium and on the bench. At the final whistle, faced with a long walk back to the city (tear gas had filled the metro stations) we did as other Liverpool fans were doing and formed an ad hoc group of about fifteen people to protect ourselves as we traversed the dark streets, with gangs of youth loitering in the shadows, ready to pick off any stragglers for their phones and watches.

The real story would get out more quickly this time, and that day became an instance where one was glad to have the presence of pervasive and decentralized social media. Real-time commentary and video made clear what was going on and made it easier to understand who was at fault. But it was also a reminder that, decades after Heysel and Hillsborough, after the worst excesses of British football hooliganism had been effectively banned from stadia, and when the entirety of fan culture occupied a different and more positive cultural space ... the police in many European countries (including France, Spain, and Italy) still treated football fans—*especially* English football fans—like cattle. It was infuriating.

UEFA ultimately apologized for its mishandling. Those who filed a class-action suit (myself included) got the cost of their tickets refunded.

During my time at Liverpool, I was proud and humbled by the enthusiasm, the generosity of spirit, the intelligence, and the loyalty of our fans. But I was never prouder of our supporters than I was that day in Paris. They were stellar when faced with reprehensible circumstances. If it had been followers of a different club, it could have been a far different outcome.

◆

I did not have long to dwell on the debacle that was Paris. Just a few days later, I embarked on the dream vacation. I had been to the Serengeti with Debbie in 2018, and we loved it so much, we agreed we should return one day with all our children. So I set out planning a trip which would bring together my three children with Bernice, Debbie's two sons, Remy and Brodie, and my daughter Alex. I have lived an admittedly imperfect life, but these are the people I love, and I wanted nothing more than to bring them all together for this magnificent adventure.

The traveling party, coming from New York, Los Angeles, and Liverpool, converged for the journey in Doha. From there it was a flight to Kilimanjaro and then a chartered plan to Arusha, Tanzania, where we were met by a fleet of Land Cruisers. It was the time of year of the Great Migration, the largest annual movement of land animals in the world. We ranged through the grassy lands of Tanzania, but make no mistake—we weren't roughing it. This was glamping at its most luxurious. And yet we were also out in the wild, in a way that my urbanite children could never have comprehended without experiencing it. There was a moment on the third day of the safari when we came up over a rise and saw a dazzle of zebras and a confusion of wildebeest—by the thousands, not merely hundreds. It was awe-inspiring and indescribable, but an indelible moment that would not soon be forgotten.

After five days in the outback, we spent five days in Zanzibar. I know that every one of my children had felt at times that I put my work above my quality time with them. They weren't wrong, and the fact that I was driven largely to provide for them—just as my parents had provided for me and my siblings—was both true and at some level beside the point. We live messy lives, fall in and out of love and, if we're fortunate, find the right partner in the end. Along the way, there are hurt feelings and disappointment. But I loved and was proud of all my children; Debbie felt the same about her boys. It was a trip to remember, and then, after ten memorable days, we all returned to our lives.

I had hit the ground running in California. For a time, I reunited with my old boss John Riccitiello, CEO of Unity Technologies, the global leader in game engine software, particularly for the mobile platform. We were trying to win the race to develop cutting-edge live volumetric 3-D technology. (It was a race that Unity didn't win, but the advances that we and other competitors made contributed to the next-gen capability seen in the semi-automated offside technology used at the Euros in 2024.)

But the project that took most of my time in California began with the simple act of purchasing a used car. I was at Milpas Motors in Santa Barbara in February 2021, talking to the owner, Jim Crook. When I explained my background, he smiled excitedly and said, "There's someone you've got to talk to." He picked up the phone and called his friend

Mick Luckhurst, the former kicker for the Atlanta Falcons. Luckhurst, one of the first British players in the NFL, had grown up in Hertfordshire and was a Manchester United fan. We hit it off immediately, forgiving each other our respective loyalties. One of the first things he told me was that there was someone *else* I had to meet. That turned out to be Tim Vom Steeg, the legendary head coach of the men's soccer program at University of California Santa Barbara. The three of us met over coffee one day, and shared stories of the dark ages for US soccer. I'd remembered Santa Barbara being a hotbed of youth soccer during my days driving around the state for Patrick. It was a certainty that a few pairs of the Patrick shoes I sold to Copeland Sports in Santa Barbara were subsequently purchased by Tim in his playing days.

At the end of the conversation, Tim and Mick talked about the potential of Santa Barbara as a city for the United Soccer League, the national secondary league that operates in dozens of different cities across the country, at a level just below Major League Soccer. They eventually put me in touch with USL deputy CEO Justin Papadakis and COO Dan Holman, whom I met at the Hilton on the waterfront in Santa Barbara. They confirmed what Mick and Tim had told me: The USL was eager to tap into the Santa Barbara market but hadn't found the right ownership group to make it happen. At the end of a long and compelling meeting, I told them, "Look, I'll help. I will be an engaged *minority* owner. I believe in this. And the experience I've just had in Liverpool validates what I've always known is the power of this game to bring joy and happiness and bring people together."

Over the next couple months I connected with some others in the community who had expressed an interest, and I waited for someone to take the reins. A lot of people sounded excited, but nothing happened. After a few more weeks, the situation became clear to me. The launch of civic-wide support for a soccer team was not going to happen with a bunch of volunteers. You can't do this in your spare time with well-intentioned soccer moms and dads. They are crucial once you get off the ground, but they can't get the enterprise off the ground in the first place. Someone needed to spend money to start the process. At this point, I made a decision. Rather than rallying support around a theoretical concept, I decided to begin at the end. Create the club, fund it appropriately, give it an identity, a crest, a concept, and *then* bring that to the community.

Santa Barbara has a rich Spanish heritage. The UCSB sports teams are called the Gauchos (after the nomadic horsemen from the Argentine and Uruguayan grasslands) and the Santa Barbara City College teams are known as the Vaqueros (horse-mounted cattle herders). Tim Vom Steeg's wife, Almeria, gave me a list of possible team names. I didn't want something generic like Santa Barbara FC, nor did I want some bastardized version of a European name, like Real Santa Barbara or Santa Barbara United.

But then I saw one of the names on her list and instantly pointed to it.

"That's it!," I said. "Santa Barbara Sky."

Santa Barbara Sky.

I loved it, because it's bright and optimistic, and it's wide open for interpretation. I hired a talented, football-friendly graphic designer named Chris Payne in New York, and told him to come up with something distinctively Santa Barbara.

Payne did his homework, digging deeply into the history of the martyred Saint Barbara, who faced religious persecution when she converted to Christianity in the third century. Later canonized, her memory exudes resilience and courage in the face of adversity. Payne's brilliant rendering reimagined Saint Barbara as a glorious beacon—Statue of Liberty-esque in her iconography—and the broad contours of the crest reflected the deep windows of Spanish architecture in the area. The team colors were midnight blue and the burnt orange of terracotta, the latter evoking the Spanish tiled roofs so popular in the area.

Along with registering the name of the club, Debbie and I established and funded a charitable foundation, Fundación Cielo, to offer scholarships along with nutritional and fitness education to the youth in the area, with a particular emphasis on reaching out to the underserved portions of the Hispanic community in Santa Barbara. That March of 2022, Debbie and I hosted a gathering of Hispanic community leaders at our home, receiving universal support for the concept.

That same month, I met with the board of trustees at Santa Barbara City College. The league had been very enthusiastic about playing matches on the campus of City College, whose La Playa Stadium possessed spectacular views, looking out directly onto palm trees, beachfront, and the Pacific Ocean. La Playa was undeniably picturesque, but also had some considerable drawbacks (artificial turf, American football lines, a running track surrounding the field, deteriorating bleachers). The meeting with the City College board was surprisingly rocky, as several trustees were adamant that they didn't think professional soccer would do anything for the community or the campus. They didn't want to change a thing—the football lines, the track surrounding the field, the artificial turf—for professional soccer. But after the somewhat combative meeting, I received an email from the college that our proposed agreement had been approved by the president's cabinet at SBCC.

On July 12, 2022, we scheduled a launch party in downtown Santa Barbara, with the mayor Randy Rowse (a former rugby player, who well understood the power of sports to positively affect a community) and scores of other dignitaries, covered by local TV, radio, and print media. I announced the club's name, unveiled the club's crest, thanked Vom Steeg and Luckhurst, as well as one of the reps at City College, and announced plans to begin playing at La Playa Stadium the following year. The evening was an overwhelming success—everyone in attendance went home with Santa Barbara Sky scarves, and Debbie and I toasted a successful launch.

It wasn't until the next morning that I received an indignant phone call from City College—emphasizing that the president's cabinet approval was *not* sufficient to announce an agreement—and was ordered to appear at the next meeting of the board of trustees. After that meeting a week later, in which I faced more strident pushback, I finally accepted that this just wasn't going to work out. If the honeymoon phase was this difficult, what was going to happen when we *needed* them? I went home and wrote a letter to the board, stating in part: "Projects of this potential impact require cooperation, collaboration, and a willingness to work through the myriad challenges. As I'm sure you will agree, all stakeholders were not in agreement of the value to the community that bringing top level soccer to La Playa Stadium would generate, and as such I feel that it would be best for all parties at this juncture if we went our separate ways."

So, we had a team, we had an identity, we had a plan. But we didn't have a stadium.

Yet there was still one other viable stadium in the area, and though it was a 10-minute drive from downtown Santa Barbara, and lacked the breathtaking scenery, it did have plenty to recommend it: The largest stadium capacity in the area, no track surrounding it, no American football lines, and a natural grass field perfectly suited for soccer. Harder Stadium, located on the UCSB campus, had hosted an NCAA soccer Final Four, and had also led the nation in attendance nine times.

I called back Tim Vom Steeg. "Tim," I said. "We need to talk..."

Vom Steeg had been a great supporter of professional soccer coming to Santa Barbara, but he also recognized it would be easier if that professional soccer was elsewhere in the community, without all the inevitable challenges of sharing a field, facilities, practice time, and schedules. But Tim had come around to seeing the necessity, and the UCSB athletic director Kelly Barsky—a go-getter and the former women's basketball coach at the school—helped pave the way for the long and involved negotiation.

The stadium, built in 1966 and named after longtime UCSB football coach Spud Harder, has a rich history. When the Green Bay Packers flew to California for the first Super Bowl in 1967, Vince Lombardi wanted to keep the team as far from the distractions of LA and Hollywood as possible. So the team trained on the campus of UCSB, at the stadium.

The UCSB campus is actually located in Isla Vista, California, just down the freeway from downtown. Barsky understood the value of connecting the community of Santa Barbara to the campus of UCSB, and also appreciated our pledge to help refurbish the stadium. That eventually got done, though given the punishing trifecta of lawyers and academia and California, it of course took eighteen months. At some point it became clear we weren't going to start in 2023, and then it became clear we weren't going to start in 2024 either.

But that was just as well, because it also took me that long to find a majority investor. I had made it clear to the USL as well as the Santa Barbara soccer mafia that, though I was willing to front the money to get the enterprise started, I was not going to be the major investor. I didn't have the time and I didn't have the money. I was happy to be involved in an advisory capacity, but someone else was going to need to carry the weight. Throughout 2023 and the first part of 2024, I met probably two dozen different potential investors, many from the Santa Barbara area and others from as far away as the UK, Spain, and Germany. In the end, those all came to naught—but the appeal of the concept was too strong, the

USL leadership was too committed, and by that time, I had grown too attached. So we worked it out.

It had taken more than three years from the first time I'd been approached on the idea, but by the summer of 2024, we were on track, taking season-ticket orders for the Santa Barbara Sky. The supporters' group—they had named themselves the Terra Cotta Army—was already organized and preparing. Adding to the logistical drama, I received a call from the league in late 2024 offering us a place in the USL Championship, one league above where we had originally planned to compete, which delayed our kickoff another year. But everything was now in place, hiring the front office nearly complete, and we all could focus on finally getting on the pitch in March 2026. Professional soccer was coming to Santa Barbara.

◆

Of course, even as I was building a new American club, I never stopped loving my old English club. In January 2024, my phone started blowing up and, like so many other Liverpool fans around the world, I was saddened to see the news that Jürgen Klopp would be stepping down at the end of the season.

It was a reminder, not that I needed one, that nothing lasts forever. As I look back on the epic journey I've traveled—and at the road ahead—I realize how often football has compelled me forward. Playing it, watching it, coaching it, marketing it, selling it, managing it, and, above all—whether working in the sport or merely watching it—recognizing it as a conduit to bring people together all over the world.

In an increasingly divided world, overrun by totalitarians and authoritarians, a growing income gap between the haves and the have-nots, football is still one of the last things—maybe the very *best* thing—to bring people together. I often think of the first trip Debbie and I took to the Serengeti. It was during the World Cup of 2018, and at the end of our long days, we would sit in the tent with the guides and watch games on a tiny black-and-white TV. The guides didn't speak English, and I didn't speak Ngorome, the Bantu language indigenous to the Serengeti. But we shared the common body language of the world's most popular sport, and watched the games together in the middle of the Tanzanian jungle.

As it turns out, a goal is a goal in almost any language.

EPILOGUE

CIRCLE OF LIFE

Sometimes I'm in Dargan's, the Irish pub in Santa Barbara with dozens of fellow Reds. Sometimes I'm at home, with no one but our dogs Rocket and Raisin. Under whatever circumstances, I feel a surge of energy as I prepare to watch the Reds take on Spurs or City or United. And though I'm hard by the coast of California on a 70-degree day, I still *feel* quintessentially there.

Liverpool is, in some superficial ways, unrecognizable from the bomb-ravaged city I was born into nearly seventy years ago. The barrow girls may no longer push their carts through the streets, but the eternal verities of their lives remain an indelible part of the DNA of those from Merseyside. Liverpool has always been a city where hardship is met with hustle, and where the determination to move forward—no matter the obstacle—remains the cornerstone of its identity.

Though the city is resplendent today, a mixture of modern and timeless, that same grit and determination courses through the veins of Liverpudlians. From the dock workers who ensure the ports remain a vital artery of trade, to the creative minds driving the city's cultural revival in places like the Baltic Triangle, the ethic of unyielding hard work persists. Just as those women kept the wheels of daily life turning, modern Liverpudlians continue to push forward—innovating, creating, and building on the foundation laid by generations past, aided by the quick wit and warmth that sets Scousers apart, in my biased opinion, from inhabitants of other cities in the UK. If the British are known for being standoffish, too clever by half, people from Liverpool are the *least* British of all.

It's a long way from the raw, rainy streets of postwar Liverpool to the sun and smooth surfaces of twenty-first-century California. There are numerous things about my life today— from the Peloton to the iPhone, self-driving cars to "smart" refrigerators—that would have seemed like pure science fiction to the young Peter Moore.

As I near my 70th birthday, I'm keenly aware of the passage of time, and the inevitability of change. I've learned enough to make my peace with it. I don't ever want to be one of those people grumbling that everything used to be better. Because I know that in countless ways, modern life has gotten so much safer and humane.

At the same time, I remain committed to the principles that prevail across the eras. Family remains hugely important, and it gives me great satisfaction when I return to the UK to find my siblings all settled and happily living on the same street, just across the road from where my mum and dad spent their retirement, and one well-struck free kick away from the Red Lion, which is itself much changed but still bearing the same name.

And just as I would have loved for my father to see me on the Champions League parade route following Liverpool's win in Madrid, I've derived immense pleasure from watching my children distinguish themselves in their lives and careers.

Tara navigated her way through the demanding PR trenches at Rogers & Cowan and Edelman, then worked for nearly five years at Under Armour, when that company was trying to slay the goliath Nike just as Reebok had tried to when I was there in the '90s. She's now the director of global integrated communications for Electronic Arts, where she directly oversees the marketing and brand positioning of the Sims and Skate franchises. I couldn't be prouder of the confident, engaging, and amazingly kind-hearted woman she has become

Tyler—who has gaming in his DNA—worked his way up to national sales director during his eleven years at IGN Entertainment. Today he's the account director of gaming at the company Future, and I've known very few people who had a better grasp of the ineffable elements that can lift a particular game from a pastime to a passion and bring external brands into that world. While he loves his work, he's also found happiness in his personal life with his wife Angela.

Toni-Marie was already preternaturally mature when she was doing internships while attending the University of San Francisco. In less than a decade, she's worked her way up from an entry-level position to senior sales marketing manager for Electronic Arts, based out of New York City. I love our almost daily interactions on business challenges she might be facing that day, and I am perpetually in awe of her professionalism, work ethic, and love of life, both professional and personal. Of course, Bernice deserves credit for each of their successes, as she did so much of the hands-on parenting.

And then there's Alexandra, who braved traveling overseas to find work in Liverpool, and did so working for a prestigious law firm, as well as volunteering as the marketing director of the Peter Moore Foundation, and persevered even as she arrived in the midst of the Covid madness, only to learn that I was preparing to return to the States. She remained on Merseyside and thrived. In 2024, she landed a full-time job as a community marketing manager at the LFC Foundation. I was disappointed that I couldn't be there in Liverpool with her, but she has shone on her own terms.

It was true that, in each case, my children found an initial opportunity because I was able to open a door for them. But then each one had to succeed or fail on his or her own merits, knowing that they would face additional pressure and scrutiny along the way. And it is a source of immense pride and humility that they all have excelled, sharing much of the work ethic that I inherited from my own parents. They are vibrant, caring, self-reliant young adults. And the fact that they are doing just what they should be doing—charting their course, making lives of their own—means I don't see any of them as often as I'd like.

Each child is wonderfully unique, but they do share one commonality: They are Americans, and over the decades it's clear that I've become one myself, and not just in name. I love England, and will always remain connected to my hometown of Liverpool. (In the summer of 2024, I even got decked out in full Sgt. Pepper garb—McCartney's blue suit— to take Debbie to the final showing of *The Beatles Love* by Cirque du Soleil at the Mirage in Las Vegas.) But by disposition and temperament, by outlook and optimism, by character and core values, I have become an American, in more than just my passport designation. The success I've found, on both sides of the Atlantic, wouldn't have happened if I hadn't done that least British of all things—rolled the dice and risked it all.

That's also how I wound up with my life partner. Debbie indeed looks like the quintessential tanned, upbeat, effervescent California Girl, but her merits go far deeper. I'll never forget how gracefully she stepped into her role at Liverpool—a high-visibility, high-pressure role as my wing woman—and then went beyond that to carve out her own niche, with the LFC Foundation and Red Neighbours. We've been back in the States for four years, but every Monday she's still on Zoom, leading the Liverpool ladies in chair yoga, as well as continuing to serve on the charity committee for the Clatterbridge Cancer Hospital.

Now back on her home turf, in Santa Barbara, she is the executive director of Fundacion Cielo. And she's been instrumental in the outreach to the community, turning this idea we had into a tangible success.

Like me, she has a deep grounding in both tech and sports, which makes her a perfect partner, both personally and professionally. There are very few things I do that I don't bounce off her first. Her sensibilities and values are similar to my own. In sum, I've got the reassurance of finding a wife whose worldview I share. But also the sense that every day is a new adventure.

To that point, while putting the finishing touches on this book, I was reminded of the adventures that the passage of time delivers. We are at a time in our history when technology is under the spotlight for understandable reasons, where the looming prospect of the artificial intelligence revolution threatens to put millions of people out of work. There are valid concerns on multiple fronts, but it's also worth noting the way that advances in technology can make life better, and even save some lives in the process.

On a Friday morning in July 2024, I was going about my business as normal, prior to driving to Santa Barbara Airport to pick up my daughter Tara, who was staying with us for a few days. As I moved around, I felt a little lightheaded and had an unusual shortness of breath. Being a typical stubborn, bull-headed male, I thought little of it and instead opted to stop for a latte at Starbucks on the way to the airport. Liquid jump-start! That'll knock me back into shape!

I was sitting in the cell lot at the airport when I started to receive notifications from my Apple Watch. It had been tracking my heartbeats per minute (BPM) over the past couple of hours and was concerned with a radical drop down to 30 over the past twenty minutes. That got my attention, and my stubbornness gave way to a call to Debbie. With her prior work at FitBit, she was fully conversant with health-related data, and she acted decisively. She jumped in her car and collected me from the airport, leaving a car there for Tara.

Within minutes we were at the Santa Barbara Cottage Hospital, where I was admitted and rolled into an examination room. I was descended upon by an assured "crash team" that within seconds had me prodded, probed, and hooked up to monitors, which immediately started printing out an electrocardiogram. Literally within two minutes, the ER doctor ran in, rather theatrically waving the ECG printout, shouting, "This is not good! This is not good! You are going to need a pacemaker!" Once calmness was regained in the room, I was informed that I was in complete heart block, meaning my electrical system had failed and the upper and lower chambers had ceased communicating with each other, resulting in greatly reduced blood flow and by then a BPM of 24.

I was prepped for surgery and went into theater within a couple of hours. I say theater but it was more like a command center, with multiple screens above the gurney which would monitor heart and vitals and also guide the electrocardiologist as he inserted the device, and the technician from Abbott, the manufacturer of the pacemaker, as they "paced" my heart before they felt confident that they had calibrated the device to the point it could take over keeping me alive.

Forty-eight hours later I felt great. A little sore where the device was sitting, but other than that back to normal and thoroughly enjoying a healthy 65 BPM. If my Apple Watch, bless it, hadn't been politely insistent about the gravity of my condition, I doubt I'd be here today. Technology rightly needs to be controlled and monitored, but in this case, it was a literal lifesaver.

Five days later, we were back at Santa Barbara Cottage Hospital, where we lost Debbie's mom, Molly, at the age of 91. She leaves a big hole in our blended family, and will be badly missed.

◆

But in the end, I keep coming back to the football, and what it can do.

In Santa Barbara, an area of the country with vast diversity in wealth, housing, racial makeup, and political views, the build-up to the 2026 debut of the Sky was encouraging for all the ways it was blurring those differences, bringing different elements of the community together.

These people may not agree on politics, or climate change, or whether downtown Santa Barbara needs more bike lanes, but they are proud of their city, and eager to unite behind a club that will represent it. And in achieving the framework for the club, that sense of American ingenuity—of bright people trying to find a way to make things better, leaning into solutions rather than viewing any roadblock as intractable—was essential.

In the end, as so often happens when the best elements of idealism and pragmatism come together, the solution turned out to help everyone involved. What I needed most was a bona fide stadium for the Santa Barbara Sky to play in. What UC Santa Barbara needed was a way to have a more assured and reliable connection with its namesake city, after decades as the red-headed stepchild, an afterthought located ten minutes down the 101 in Isla Vista. The solution that emerged helped our club, helped the university, and helped the city. In the process, the shared love of the game continued to open doors that I couldn't have imagined: The incorrigible ManU fan Mick Luckhurst, the soccer lifer and legendary coach Tim vom Steeg, the visionary UCSB athletic director Kelly Barsky.

At the Sky, we have the benefit of Sheralyn Baltes, who seems to already know and be friends with everyone in the city. I was introduced to Sheralyn in early 2022 and hired her almost immediately, as the Sky's senior vice-president for technology and business operations. As president of the Santa Barbara Soccer Club, she was already plugged into the city's soccer scene. She'd also played the game in college, at the University of Montana, and was a soccer mom herself. All of which made her exactly the right person for the early work we needed to do to get the club off the ground.

It's not only that the sport brings people together. It does so in ways that were unimaginable a couple of generations ago. In the realm of good news that's rarely reported, I'd raise up the change in the culture of football fandom over the past fifty years. Not only in England, but over much of the world, the oppressively male and often hostile and racist ethos—so tribal and violent in its particulars that it was viewed as a stain on the nation—has been rebuilt and reimagined, as a tolerant and egalitarian society, open to all who wish to join.

Forty years ago, I wrote my thesis as part of the completion of my master's degree at Cal State Long Beach. It was entitled *More Than a Game: The Impact of Soccer on British Society.* My writing was focused on the subculture of hooliganism surrounding the game at that period, and the rabid territorialism and tribalism that ravaged and stained the game in the '70s and '80s. But with the advent of better stadium conditions, more thoughtful policing techniques, and with calmer heads eventually prevailing, this blight on the game is, for the most part, generally behind us. My opening paragraph in that thesis was plucked from the Harrow School Song, written in 1872:

God gave us bases to guard or beleaguer
Games to play out whether serious or fun
Fights for the fearless or goals for the eager
Twenty or thirty or forty years on

Times have changed, but the competitive juices that flow within us remain. The fans of the world's game are as passionate as they ever were, but maybe there are more things to worry about now than just wins and losses, great goals and spectacular saves. I for one do not yearn for what some see as the good old days of muddy pitches, fights before, during, and after the match, and the poisonous culture rampant in those dilapidated football grounds of yesteryear.

For example, this new iteration of fan culture isn't only not racist, it's *anti-racist* and inclusive in spirit. During my days on the Kop during the 1970s, it would have been unimaginable that I'd take my wife there someday. But I did, and it was wonderful.

The game isn't a panacea. It can't whip inflation, or solve income inequality, or erase racism. What it can do, across seasons and tournaments, is serve as a prism through which people—even as they are locked into the eternal sporting dichotomy of them and us—see the humanity of other people, throughout the country and throughout the world.

You don't have to be a native of Senegal or Japan to have been touched by the scenes from the 2018 World Cup of those nations' fans cleaning up their sections in the stadiums after matches, rather than just marching off to the pub. You don't have to be from Denmark to appreciate the miracle of Christian Eriksen, who died on the field during the European Championships in 2021, coming back to score a goal in the 2024 European Championships. And you didn't have to be from France to appreciate the words of Kylian Mbappe and Ibrahima Konate in the days leading up to the final round of French elections in 2024, which may well have gone some distance in pulling the country away from Marine Le Pen and her far-right leadership.

Finally, you don't have to have been at Anfield on that immense, magical night against Barcelona in 2019 to have learned its signal lesson: If people are committed and united, and feel supported, nearly any feat is possible. As the injured Mo Salah's T-shirt boldly proclaimed as he watched from the sidelines: Never Give Up.

The game taught me this truth, and so many others. Did I have any sense that the choice I made in 1959—a football match or half a crown—would set my life on a definite course? No, but I could have guessed one thing: Attending a football match would remain a joy throughout my life, and those myriad pleasures would often connect me back to that day in November 1959.

So it was on a sun-drenched July afternoon in California. I was walking into Harder Stadium for the big event of the summer in Santa Barbara—the friendly between AFC Bournemouth and Wrexham AFC, the team of my youth. The success of Rob and Ryan's endeavors and the *Welcome to Wrexham* TV series had created a fertile market for Wrexham to play summer friendlies in the US. And because the AFC Bournemouth owner Bill Foley had roots in Santa Barbara, Bournemouth and Wrexham would play a game here, to be nationally televised. I saw Rob before the game started, and he invited Debbie and me over to his hospitality tent. We hugged and gave each other a look that all but screamed, "Can you believe this!?!"

We wanted to go back to our pre-assigned seats to watch the game, and so headed toward the main stand when I was stopped by a vision: A father walking hand in hand with his young son, no more than four or five. We wound up in the same concession line, and chatted for a minute. They had driven in from Oxnard to see the game, which was the boy's very first live soccer match. I couldn't help but think of my four-year-old self, small hand in my father's grip, walking wide-eyed and innocent up to the gates at Anfield. In a sense, the game that hooked me that day in Liverpool had brought me here, 5,301 miles away, a pilgrim in a new land.

Perhaps that boy and his dad would forge their bond through the Beautiful Game. It might be the defining event in his life. Or it could just be a grand day out, which was fine as well. The possibilities were endless. All I know for sure was that, as he looked out on the pitch, he felt connected to something wondrous.

Sixty-five years after my first match, I knew exactly how he felt. And one of the blessings of my life is that I *still* feel that way.

ACKNOWLEDGMENTS

Writing *Game Changer* has been as much a journey of gratitude as it has been a reflection on my life.

I would not have had a story to tell were it not for the influence of my mum and dad, whose courage and determination gave me a foundation. Additionally, I'm grateful for the inspiration and direction of O.M. Edwards, the resilient optimism of Eddie Robinson, and the generous hospitality of the entire Bokanyi family.

My own story has been shaped by many others, and in some cases it's the others who know the story better. Our de facto family historian is my brother Andy, whose sense of recall and specificity—about the sights and sounds of our little corner of Wales—remains pin-sharp. The book is better because of the clarity of his memory. I'm also grateful for the shared memories of Andy's wife Sharon, my brother Phil and his wife Judith, my sister Emma and her husband Andrew Evans. In putting together the puzzle pieces of my early life, I'm also grateful to Chris and Lynne Marsden, Beth Bokanyi Holmes, Brian Knowles, Eddie Robinson, Mike Fischer, David Holland, Tim Booth, Tina Roberts, Lori Labrie, John Riccitiello, Robbie Bach, Kathleen Joyce, Steve Rotheram, Andy Cooke, David and Sharon Telling, C.J. Collins, John McCluskey, Steve Graham, Emma Rodgers and John Mok, and Hugh and Cathy Frost.

Others have played a key role over the years, and I'm grateful to Bill Gates, Steve Ballmer, Paul Fireman, Tana Billingsley, Bernie Stolar, David Tinson, Andrew Wilson,

Billy Hogan, Andy Hughes, Susan Black, Pete Price, Andy Parker, Sheralyn Baltes, Paul Cairns, Todd Sitrin, Jeff Brown, Michael Parkinson, Phil Thompson, John Aldridge, Ian Rush, Sir Kenny Dalglish, John Barnes, Jamie Carragher, Gary McAllister, and Robbie Fowler.

My thanks as well to Bernice Moore, an amazing mother who has indomitably shaped our children into the wonderful adults they have become; to Tara, Tyler, and Toni-Marie Moore, about whom I couldn't be prouder or more in awe of what they have achieved in life so far; and to Alexandra Robertson, who has surmounted so many obstacles in life and has emerged as a bright adult with so much promise.

Special thanks to Alison Welsby and the entire staff at Liverpool University Press for their feedback and help in bringing my story to print. And to my sounding board, Michael MacCambridge. Your wisdom, expertise, and gentle but firm guidance on content helped guide me through this journey of putting my fragmented thoughts and anecdotes together in a readable format. I am forever in your debt.

And finally, this book wouldn't have been written—and couldn't have had such a happy ending—without Debbie Moore, my lighthouse and shining beacon of can-do optimism. You light up every corner of my life with your energy and undying support. Thank you for being by my side through all the ups and downs of our incredible adventure together.

—PM, Montecito, February 2025